Intermissions for Hope
Spiritual Moments for Spiritual Renewal

Julie Crane

ISBN-10: 150273477X
ISBN-13: 978-1502734778

DEDICATION

… do it all for the glory of God. – 1 Corinthians 10:31

ACKNOWLEDGMENTS

JESUS, my Lord.

Kathy Bruins, successful author/editor in her own right, both family and friend to me, the greatest encourager, who dreams big, believes big, celebrates big

My husband Scott, who holds me close everyday, yet lets me spread my wings and fly

Do not despair (lose heart)

Perplexed, but not in despair (2 Corinthians 4:8).

Perplexed: puzzled, at a loss, confused; mystified, baffled, bewildered

Despair: misery, hopelessness, anguish, gloom, lose heart

Studying these two words, you'd think one may be just an extreme case of the other. Perplexed appears to mean some level of distress, but there is still time for something right to happen. Where despair impresses upon us a sense that all options appear to have been exhausted and there is no good resolution in sight.

I stumbled across this verse shortly after reading about Jesus walking on the water. A fabulous rescue, wouldn't you say? He's been out healing people left and right. He just fed 5,000. His friends were out in a boat on the stormy sea, and Jesus came right to them walking on the water. But you need to read those verses a little closer. Because what I realized and found out, was that several hours past between the guys in the boat in the storm and when Jesus came across on the waters. These two events are three verses apart. Yet in Matthew 14:22, the disciples were told to get in the boat in the early evening (6:00 p.m.), and in verse 25, Jesus came to them during the fourth watch (3:00 – 6:00 a.m.). This means they were fighting the storm for nine, ten or more hours on their own. Where was Jesus? Hours went by. Surely, He knew. They must have questioned … wondered. Did they panic under these circumstances? Were they simply perplexed (baffled, mystified, bewildered), or did they lose heart (despair) that Jesus would not ever come?

Can you imagine the anxiety level? Even when He does come, the Bible says they are terrified. It's only when He steps into the boat with them that everything calms down and they worship Him saying, "Truly You are the Son of God."

Are you at a place in life where you are waffling between perplexed and despair? Are you closing in on terrified? Do not live without hope. Jesus will come. He will get right into the boat with you. *Take heart!* He says. I overcome anything this world dishes out (John 16:33). You, too, can know as the disciples did that "Truly You are the Son of God!"

Exchanging anxieties for peace

Do not be anxious about anything (Philippians 4:6).

Yeah, we've all heard *those* words before. Do not be anxious. Totally impossible, right? *God, do You have any idea the kind of day I've had? A litany of struggles, challenges and unanswered questions come to mind, right?*

Do not be anxious about anything (without Me)—

in every situation, by prayer present your requests to God (Philippians 4:6).

You see, it is not God's plan that you go through life feeling alone. In sorrows and in joys, God wants to be there for you. He doesn't want you handling everything on your own. You were created to be with God. It is a lie that God only wants to see and hear from you when you're full of praise and thanksgiving. It is His desire to have you share everything with Him. Isn't that what this verse says? In every situation, go talk to God, and His Word comes with a promise:

> *And the peace of God which transcends all understanding, will guard your hearts and your minds in Christ Jesus. (v. 7)*

The Living Bible translates it like this:

> *If you do this, you will experience God's peace, which is far more wonderful than the human mind can understand. His*

peace will keep your thoughts and your hearts quiet and at rest as you trust in Christ Jesus.

I can't explain how that happens; I can just testify that it *does* happen. I pray about some stressful concern and it's like a poison oozes out. God fills that void with some kind of assurance that it's going to somehow work out. He's powerful like that. Not even my most humongous, overwhelming fear stops Him from reaching me with some kind of comforting word. Sometimes, it's a piece of a Scripture verse that I mysteriously recall. At times, it's a line of a song being played in the background. Other times, it is a thought expressed in a devotional or a book I am reading. He reaches me. He knows how to calm me down and grant me rest. It's amazing to me that He can do that without even changing my circumstances. *HE* expands my trust in Him, and by His mercy and grace, if I get anxious again, I can go talk to Him again. I can trust that He will calm me down again—even if it's about the same thing. God is like that. He is ready for you to rest in Him. Every time you turn to Him, you can receive. Trade your anxious thoughts for His peace right now.

Unto the Lord

Don't fret or worry. Instead of worrying, pray. Let petitions and praises shape your worries into prayers, letting God know your concerns. Before you know it, a sense of God's wholeness, everything coming together for good, will come and settle you down. It's wonderful what happens when Christ displaces worry at the center of your life (Philippians 4:6-7 THE MSG).

O dear God, here I am, trying to spend some focused time with You. Trying to desire a more loving, "can't live a minute without thoughts of You" kind of life, instead of praying to You an "I want" list every morning and scratching it off some mental to-do list before going on with my day—my way. I feel guilty for not loving You as great as You deserve. I should be consumed by Your awesomeness.

The furnace kicks in. The sunlight streams in through the window. The scent of vanilla caramel tea wafts through the room. I have the whole day before me to get some things done. Time for work. Time for play, Time for rest. And I pray this day isn't lived out as a clanging cymbal (1 Corinthians 13:1), but in whatever I do, may it be as unto You, Lord (1 Corinthians 10:31), and not unto man. Lord, if I become anxious about anything, may I calmly turn to You and just tell You what's on my mind. You are great, all-wise, all-knowing, all-present, all-powerful and have chosen to call me Your child. I am safe under the protection of Your love in a way I've never known. Truly I am safe. Truly I am protected. Worries and fears do not have to dictate the direction of my life. The God of the universe has chosen to and desires to tend to my every need. Lord, I will seek You with my whole heart. You are worthy of my trust. It is safe to share every kind of thought and feeling with You. I will not curl up in a ball and lie stagnant in condemnation. For You came to save the world (John 3:16-17). And I am saved. I will live today saved. To the honor, glory, blessing, praise of You, God. Amen.

Journal a couple of your own thoughts ...

Two-way conversation

The sheep that are My own hear and are listening to My voice; and I know them, and they follow Me. (John 10:27)

I know that there have been plenty of conversations regarding if God hears our prayers. We pray and pray and don't seem to get an answer. Right?

But in God's Word, we read and trust that He *does* hear. Remember poor ol' Hagar out in the wilderness (Genesis 21:14-20). Her and her son, Ishmael, are dying. But God hears the boy's cries, and He responds. So we know, God hears.

The thing I sometimes wonder and worry about is if I hear God? Do I ask Him for guidance or direction and wonder if I will actually hear Him? Is there anything in the Bible that gives me hope that somehow, *somehow*, I will hear Him when He responds, as Hagar did?

The answer is yes. Like Hagar, you *are* capable of hearing His voice. He, Who has promised to cheer and to guide, you will hear Him.

It's another one of those supernatural, divine, miraculous things taken care of by God. You just need to settle down and listen; don't shrug off the first thing that comes to mind just because you think it's impossible.

Write your question to God down on a piece of paper. Then write down everything that comes to mind after that—stupid or not. Write all these thoughts down for a few minutes. You might just surprise yourself with an answer from God Himself.

Journal a couple of your own thoughts ...

Little ol' mustard seed

And He (Jesus) could hardly accept the fact that they wouldn't believe in Him (Mark 6:6 – TLB).

Another version says, *"… their lack of faith distressed Him so."*

Do you think that faith the size of a mustard seed is more than enough? Are you sometimes guilty of not even having that much? Even when things were/are miraculously healed immediately, you may raise the bar and wonder if God will do <u>this next thing</u>. When He has been faithful for forever in meeting your greatest needs, your greatest one, in fact: a Savior. Someone in which you can have an on-going relationship. Are you wondering what God will do for you now? Or *if* He'll do?

I've seen examples of His answers in safe travels on a snowy road, job placements, and cancer survivors. We read that sins are forgiven and people get up and walk (Mark 2:9). I've seen people rally around the poor and needy and the brokenhearted.

In this world, you will have trouble. But take heart! (John 16:33)

He gives you His peace and strength to persevere towards that certain hope. God can do and will do and does do … miracle upon miracle …

What if I gathered up all the miracles in my life and you gathered up all of yours, and all our friends did the same? Can you imagine the overflow of power coming down from heaven? I am reminded of the woman touching Jesus' clothes in the crowd and power went out from Him. He felt it. She felt it, and was freed from her suffering (Mark 5:27).

From before your labor and delivery to long after your release from this life to the next, God is your Sustainer. He will uphold you with His mighty right hand (Isaiah 41:10). He Who raised Jesus from the dead (for you) will certainly raise you up and strengthen you and hold you up in whatever you face today (Ephesians 1: 19-20).

Get a mustard seed and hold it between your two fingers. Press into it every day and believe in His resurrection power.

Your life-threatening disease

But God demonstrates His own love for us in this: While we were still sinners, Christ died for us (Romans 5:8).

Your child is diagnosed with a life-threatening disease. After all the emotional upheaval, you go to a specialist. You discuss treatment options. You try one after another. More doctors are added, too. Prayer chains are activated. You Google and research and study, draining every financial resource. You begin fundraisers, and will do anything and everything no matter the cost. *This precious life must be saved from the jaws of death!* Some would even pray to trade places. "Take me instead!" You'll do anything. Pay any price.

So it is with your Father in heaven. God finds you, His precious child, filled with a deadly disease—sin. And God does, just like you, anything to save you from hell, so you will be with Him forever. He knows the steep price. Blood. Death. But He comes down Himself, God in the flesh, and pays it. Pays for it all. "Take Me instead," could have easily been Jesus' last words. You (insert your name) are *that* precious in His sight.

So no more guilt and shame about this. You wouldn't want your child feeling like that because you exhausted your savings, retirement fund, sold house and home—everything gone to ensure recovery and restored life. Now is the time for rejoicing: eternal life is purchased and promised! Absolute and all-encompassing forgiveness, release, freedom has been granted. God sees His precious child in life-threatening danger and out of His great love <u>just has to do something!</u>

O dear God, thank You, for the ultimate, perfect, complete rescue from the eternal doom of a sinful life. Thank You for washing the disease of sin all away. Thank You for preparing a place for us where sin, death and the devil are no more. In our great Savior's Name, Amen.

God's daily bread

Listen for GOD's voice in everything you do, everywhere you go; He's the one who will keep you on track (Proverbs 3:6 THE MSG).

I was feeling guilty, because as important as it is to read your Bible every day, I haven't been doing it every day. It's not because I'm overly busy either. I simply got interested/busy/distracted in doing other things. I usually read my Bible in the mornings. So when other things happen at that time of day, I find that it just doesn't "feel" right to do it *later on.*

God doesn't want us feeling guilty. In fact, He opened my eyes today on some of the other ways I have been connecting with Him and His Word.

For instance, I recently joined an online diet coaching program, and the leader talked about how believers get a new, clean spirit but not a new, clean flesh. So my flesh is always going to be trying to tell me what to do based on feelings (I don't feel like exercising; I don't feel like drinking more water, I don't feel like reading my Bible) But I have a new, clean spirit within me now and *that* spirit gives me the *desire* to obey God despite my feelings.

When I obey with good choices, I am rewarded. It makes me think of something in the Bible about the sinful nature having its mind set on what *that* nature desires, but those who live according to the Spirit have their hearts set on what the Spirit desires (see Romans 8:5-11)

I'm also reading an interesting Christian novel where one of the characters talks about not giving up or doubting God, no matter what.

Don't you dare doubt or question His character. God is always present, God is always working for good on your behalf. Trust Him no matter what. I am reminded of verses in the Bible that talk about nothing being too difficult for Him, and that His plans are better and greater than my own.

God finds me and feeds me His "daily bread." Many times, it's from the Bible reading I do in the morning. Sometimes He has other ways of causing me to think on Him. His Word comes to me and speaks to me. Today, it was through an email and a fictional piece. I was able to recall some basic concepts from God's Word. Knowing God and His Word doesn't mean you have to have the verses all memorized, but that you remember the message and meaning. You see, He does take care of us; He does lead, guide, direct our steps. He does provide, sustain, encourage, and equip.

Miracle musings

Read Mark 2:1-12.

This is the story of Jesus healing a paralytic. Following, are some notes I wrote in my journal while reading this story. I paused, stopped and reflected at various spots and pondered over different phrases:

> *... the people heard that He had come home. So many gathered that there was no room left, not even outside the door (verse 2)*

O dear Lord, I pray that word of Your presence would be heard and felt and that many would gather.

Many kinds of people were there from teachers of the law to paralytics listening to what Jesus had to say. Was there judgment, sideways glances, or segregation? It sounds like everybody was crowded together, singles, couples and groups of every kind; united in wanting to hear Jesus, despite their history, present condition or position.

O Lord, I pray, that we too, could come together – different in many ways but united in desiring to hear from Christ.

> *... immediately Jesus knew in His spirit (verse 8)*

O Lord, I pray that we would be so in tune with You that we would know in spirit as well; that we would know You that well and immediately be moved in our spirit.

Two miraculous God-things occur: He tells them their sins are forgiven, and to get up and walk. Jesus does indeed have such authority, because it happened. If both are equally miraculous, and He causes the paralytic to get up and walk, then He must also be able to make sins forgiven.

> *... in full view of them all (verse 12).*

Remember that so many gathered that there was no room left, not even outside the door. All these different people with different levels of spiritual belief see the paralytic get up and walk, in full view of them all. If you had been there, could anything change your mind about what you saw with your own eyes? Especially, if a lot of other people confirm it! If Jesus does one miracle, can He do two, or more? Have you ever seen anything like this? Is anything too difficult for God?

More power

But someone more powerful than I will come (Luke 3:16).

Mornings are when I often read my Bible. The New International Version (NIV) is what I have. Sometimes a phrase will catch my eye and I want to see how it is written in other translations. We are fortunate that we have the computer and with a stroke of a key or two, many various translations pop-up on the screen. So this morning, I was reading about John preparing the way in Luke 3: 16:

- *"But someone more powerful than I will come" (NIV) "… someone is coming soon who has far higher authority than mine" (LB) "He Who is mightier than I is coming" (AMP) "… someone who is much greater than I" (GNB) "… someone who is greater, so much greater" (NLT)*

You get the idea? You read that same phrase, that same concept over and over, and it starts to settle down in your mind. It starts to take root. What wonderful good news these few little words bring! I am reminded of a song that proclaims: Hallelujah! He is coming! Hallelujah! He is here!

Further along in today's reading, I find Jesus healing many. Look up Luke 4:36 and find even more hope:

With authority and power He gives orders to evil spirits and they come out!

The Message says it like this: *Someone Whose words make things happen.*
Someone Who orders demonic spirits to get out and they go!

You got demons? You got bad habits, bad attitudes, bad defaults that
you just can't shake? Feeling chained, bound, and unable to change?
Read the words of Luke 3:16 and 4:36 again proclaiming the power
of Jesus. He's the same yesterday, today and forevermore.

Journal a couple of your own thoughts ...

I can't, but…

They did not conquer by their own strength and skill, but by Your mighty power and because You smiled upon them and favored them (Psalm 44:3).

God doesn't need us. Yes, you read that right. God doesn't need us to accomplish His plans. He doesn't require us to use our finite minds and limited skills and abilities. God uses us when we come to the end of ourselves and the only wisdom and strength left available to draw from is His. This is usually when we throw in the towel and quit. We draw the line and say, "I can't." We stop right when God is going to pick up the ball. Just when things were going to get good. How many times have we missed that victorious moment because we quit? Have you thrown your hands up in surrender only to focus on the doom and gloom of your exasperation? God, the Father, loves you. Jesus, His Son, rescues you from sin, death and the devil and brings you His peace. And His Spirit arrives on the scene to bring you wisdom and strength. Surrender in the knowledge that God has got you covered. His best will show up for you. Rest in that belief, because God *will* show up. Change your "I can't" statement with "I can't on my own, but God is here and He will be my Strength."

A golden nugget

Then the LORD said to Moses, "Stretch out your hand toward the sky so that darkness spreads over Egypt—darkness that can be felt." So Moses stretched out his hand toward the sky, and total darkness covered all Egypt for three days. No one could see anyone else or move about for three days. Yet all the Israelites had light in the places where they lived (Exodus 10:21-23).

There have been times when I've tried to commit to reading "X" number of chapters in the Bible every day. I understand the importance of reading things in context and not just going to favorite passages all the time. But then I come across a verse that stops me in my tracks. A golden nugget of truth. If I'm so focused on getting my "assignment" done, I miss out on what I truly seek: "God, speak to me."

Such was the case with today's reading. Here I find a world of people caught in deepest darkness and unable to control or escape it. If you watch the evening news, it's not hard to imagine days of doom, gloom and fear. Yet God's children, the Israelites, had light in the places where they lived. Now just think about that a minute. God's children (like you and me) had light (hope, good news, freedom from deep, dark fear) in whatever place (circumstances) they lived. Life without the knowledge of Christ's presence must surely be dark and dank. But knowledge in your heart of His constant power, love, presence ... well, doesn't that ease your troubled mind? Thanks be to God for His mercy and grace to His children (you and me).

Building memories with God

God did this so that they would seek Him and perhaps reach out for Him and find Him, though He is not far from any one of us. (Acts 17:27)

Have you ever prayed for something, like strength to beat a temptation or to overcome a bad habit or to get through a long-term challenge? And it seems like God has answered, because for awhile, you *are* strong enough. But here comes a brand new day (or maybe it didn't even last that long) and your strength and focus are waning. Do I have to pray for the same thing again?

I am reminded of a joke: This man and woman went to a marriage counselor and the woman remarked, "My husband never tells me he loves me!" When the counselor questioned him about it, he responded, "I told her I loved her the day we got married. If anything changes, I'll let her know."

Now I know none of us would appreciate that kind of relationship. We all like to have others be continually nurturing, sharing good feelings and kind words of love and appreciation. Right?

"Honey, will you help me with this?" "Mom, do you know how to...?" Yes, it gives us purpose and a warm fuzzy when somebody wants us. I was just thinking about a family that gathers together annually to bake Christmas cookies. Together they pitch in. Together they work through the recipe and the decorating (and the eating!).

There's something about coming together that is more warm and wonderful than being shown how to do something one time ... and then you are on your own. No fun! No connection! No laughing, sharing and creating memories to relive later on when you need a fond memory to carry you through; to give you hope for tomorrow. And let's not put relationships on hold until Christmas. Goodness, no! Let's come together often – in love, support, in living, journeying alongside one another. Hand in hand, right? Don't you love it?

And God is just asking for the same. Walk with Him as well. Talk with Him. Build memories with Him to carry you through; giving hope for tomorrow.

Victory in the Lord

For the Lord your God is the One Who goes with you to fight for you against your enemies to give you victory. (Deuteronomy 20:4)

Have you ever watched a tightrope act? The person moves forward and back, slowly, a couple steps quickly, stops to regain balance ... a step back, three steps forward. His eyes are on the goal before him. Wobbling from time to time (much to our distress!) until he reaches the end. We cheer and breathe a sigh of relief. He made it!

Sometimes my life seems to be moving like that. From the person I was to the person I was meant to be. Moving right along. Then maybe a little backsliding. Wobbling. Lots of wobbling! Trying to keep my eyes on the goal.

Each step forward is a step away from the person (character) I used to be (before the desire to live for my Lord). Too much backsliding causes me to retreat from the Christ-like person I am meant to be, right back into old habits and old beliefs. But with each step forward, I am being drawn into the habits, behaviors and character of Christ. It can also be thought of as one end being curses and one end being blessings. Forward/good choices bring us towards a life of blessings, while backward steps draws us back into opportunities for distress and curses.

Where are you? Stepping forward? Backward? Wobbling? Creating times of distress or health and goodness? Stop to regain your balance. Keep your eyes on the goal before you. And know that with Christ, you will get to the desired end (cheers, applause, victory!).

Journal a couple of your own thoughts ...

Love – past, present, future

Let marriage be held in honor (esteemed worthy, precious, of great price, and especially dear) in all things (Hebrews 13:4).

I want to love my spouse the way my friends who have lost spouses still carry love for them. There is something deep, rich and strong in the love they express in remembering their lost one. They share memories and times gone by. Little tiny things that at the time didn't mean much, some quirky little habit maybe, but forever burned into their hearts and bringing tears where there were none before.

So often, we humans slip into these day-by-day "ruts," where precious times of living together as a couple seem so ordinary, so taken for granted. But the days they are "a-passing" and today seems like the perfect day to celebrate those things that may not appear so precious and cherishable right now, but are insurmountable in value once they are gone. Gone, but not forever.

Like getting into bed together at night and snuggling with soft whispers. Dinner in front of the TV. Sitting side by side in church (I miss that). Rooting for your favorite team. Sitting in camp chairs reading in the backyard. Touching hands as you both dive into the popcorn bowl. That quick goodbye kiss every morning. Hearing the car pull in the driveway at night. A wink and a smile from across the room. These are all precious moments to gather in the heart.

Today, I'm thanking God for all that. I want to think, list and hold each precious loving thought, and be thankful I got the chance to have a life that included all that. Loving marital experiences that have passed, but not forgotten. I'm thankful for God's plan to have us reunited in heaven. It's been but a foretaste of the love feast to come. Thanks for the preview of coming attractions!

Love you, babe...

The sock story

And I am convinced and sure of this very thing, that He Who began a good work in you will continue until of day of Jesus Christ (right up to the time of His return), developing (that good work) and perfecting and bringing it to full completion in you. (Philippians 1:6)

I've always been intimidated by the prospect of knitting socks. After all, sock yarn is much thinner than regular yarn, the needles are much smaller too and they are double-pointed (stitches are capable of sliding off both ends), and working with four needles at one time – each one sticking out in a different direction looked so cumbersome. So I steered clear even though I longed to make some pretty knitted socks. But this winter, I knew I would have time on my hands, so I accepted the challenge!

And challenge it was! Whatever could go wrong, did go wrong. Wrong size needles, not the right amount of stitches, dropped stitches, lost my place in the pattern, too loose, too tight – you name it. I started over, and over, and over again. The yarn actually got thinner because I was wearing it out with my starting over. I said to myself, "Give up. You're good at other things." Naturally, the first or second (even third) time you start over, it is disappointing. But the 10th time? And more? But what I discovered is priceless:

No matter how many mistakes I made, God brought it to completion.

Despite the numerous mistakes, I made progress.

Beginning a sock became much easier. What challenged me the first few times – I could now breeze right through. Then working on the pattern changes for the heel, at first so confusing to read, became clear. The toe of the sock I actually only did twice.

I finished the first sock after try number twelve. I kid you not. But I am so proud and can't wait to begin the other one so I can wear the set.

Are you growing weary of all the mistakes you've made (or continue to make)? Learn from me. Just try again. Some of it will become easier. And you keep at it, and more and more will become smoother and make more sense. God brings things to completion. (Philippians 1:6)

Tasting and seeing

When I consider Your heavens, the work of Your fingers, the moon and the stars, which You have set in place, what is man that You are mindful of him, the son of man that You care for him?(Psalm 8:3-4)

Who tells the sun where and when to shine so brightly? Who orders the clouds where to stand and where to block the sun's burning rays ... where to let rain fall just so? Which farmers made it out to the fields even when they were fighting off some flu bug, so that produce would appear on our table today? And whose retirement plans did He direct to be put off another year so we could have experienced care and attention in some way this week?

Oh, the many details going on behind the scenes. I remember well a dinner I had at a spiritual retreat where all the guests had to eat in silence. At first, I imagined it would be unbearable. But while others were finishing up, in the silence, it dawned on me how God's hands gets the very food on my plate from farm to truck to store to retreat to me. I just sat there will an overwhelming sense that the Creator of heaven and earth brings me food.

I pray to be awakened from my slumbering lack of awareness and be more fully present, more fully aware, more fully, abundantly joy-filled by the presence of God in my daily life.

O dear Lord, I want to relish all You send and be abundantly grateful. May I become keenly aware of Your loving hands and heart. I pray for divine, transforming, renewal of my heart and mind. Nothing is too difficult for You. I am not forever set in my ways. There is hope. With You, there is always hope! Thank You for hope over the seemingly impossible.

You may have something uplifting right around the corner. I pray for eyes that see God; ears that hear God; to taste and to sense God's goodness in every thing. What a humbling, awesome thing to realize His hand is present a zillion times a day.

Where can you go where God is not? What can you taste and see that God is not producing and delivering to you this day? What kind of knowledge do you think you have without God's hand in it? What kind of love, joy, peace, patience, goodness, kindness, gentleness, faithfulness, self-control … all gifts to you, and through others to you, by God's very own divine Holy Spirit?

O dear Lord, I pray for an unending thankful, grateful, humbled-by-all-You-do heart. May I be ever conscious and overwhelmed by Your amazing outpouring of love and be satisfied, as my response should be. This day, and all days, may I truly see You and know You as my ALL IN ALL.

Enter and be safe

The Lord is my fort where I can enter and be safe; no one can follow me in and slay me. He is a rugged mountain where I hide; He is my Savior, a rock where none can reach me, and a tower of safety. He is my shield. He is like the strong horn of a mighty fighting bull. (Psalm 18:1-2 TLB)

O Lord, how I love you! For You have done such tremendous things for me.

Have you been battling? Trying and trying and trying? Are you exhausted? Temptations still hounding you? The Lord is the place to rest and be safe while you take time to recover from your efforts. Yes, He watches over you. Yes, He guards and protects His own. And He is quite aggressive about protecting His own. I've heard it said He will move heaven and earth for you. Now, isn't that something?

I like reading different translations of the Bible. This Living Bible version really struck a cord with me this morning. Phrases that caught my eye: "where *I* can enter," "no one can follow me in," "He is my Savior," ... "a tower of safety." ... When I'm feeling beat, it's wonderful to know Someone has my back so I can rest and regroup and rethink. There is a peace and a confidence that comes from that, even though circumstances may not have changed yet. It's not over. He is my Shield and also my Guide. He is my Protector, seeing me through. Thanks be to God!

Hand in hand with the Spirit

Yet a time is coming and has now come when the true worshipers will worship the Father in the Spirit and in truth for they are the kind of worshipers the Father seeks. God is spirit, and His worshipers must worship in the Spirit and in truth." (John 4:23-24)

Worship in spirit. Beyond your human ways. A turning to the Lord. Whether you know what to say or not. There is a spiritual side to you that you are not in touch with. It isn't as obvious as your physical self. But it is there. Responds in loving ways before you even think of it. Prays without you realizing it. Creates thoughts of hope without you even trying. There is a Spirit within you that expresses in "spirit words" what the human can only groan. This Spirit articulates that emotional high of praise or extreme low of pain with an unimaginable depth of understanding. Peace that passes understanding, standing in awe of a miracle, or being deeply moved by music or a spectacular view are all pieces of worshiping in spirit. Going to God in prayer without anything to offer. Running out of human words, but staying in that prayer posture anyway. Open. Available. Exclusive. Worship in spirit. Being present before God even when it doesn't look or feel like you are there. An irresistible, don't want to tear myself away presence. Because I need You, Lord, and here is the only place where it can be expressed at its fullest. Hand in hand with Your Spirit. Whatever prayer, whatever peace, whatever awe we experience, it moves between you and God through His Spirit. For God is Spirit. And so are you.

Questioning prayer

The name of the Lord is a strong tower; the righteous run to it and are safe. (Proverbs 18:10)

O Lord, I am seeking answers where they cannot be found. Forgive my lack of intentional focus on You. You are my God. Time and time again I seem to fail, to fall short of what I am supposed to do and be. There seems to be no strength in me at all. Why can't I do this? Why is it the harder I try, the harder I fall? Even when I pray, even when I cry out, why do I still sometimes fall? What am I missing here? What am I not understanding? Why all this anxiety, O my soul, when you confess to know the living Lord? Shouldn't I be at peace? Shouldn't every little bump in the road cause me to turn to Jesus in confidence? Why so little faith when I am known by the King? The King of all no less. Should not a blanket of security fall upon me, should not I be in a constant state of praise for the One Who blankets me? Why doesn't prayer always work?

Too much focus on the problem instead of the God of the present. "Grab" a Bible verse and cling to it. Repeat it over and over – frantically, slowly, in bits and pieces. Tell yourself you believe it. Tell yourself you know it to be true. Until each word or phrase is "spoken" with your very breath. Let the words wash over you and calm you down. And do this, as often as you need of it, in remembrance of Him. Lord. Savior. Yours.

So do not fear, for I am with you;

do not be dismayed, for I am your God.

I will strengthen you and help you;

I will uphold you with My righteous right hand.

Isaiah. 41:10

Journal a couple of your own thoughts ...

Praying up and settling down

In my distress I called to the Lord; I cried to my God for help. From His temple He heard my voice; my cry came before Him, into His ears. (Psalm 18:6)

I was reading my Bible the other morning and I stumbled across something. There is a passage about the Israelites moaning and groaning and crying (about their circumstance), but it didn't say they are praying or crying out to God. I read it a couple times before it sank in – they aren't crying *out to God*. But God hears their cries and is concerned about them. (Exodus 2:23-25)

I have whined and worried and admittedly, didn't ask God for intervention right away. There have been times when I have prayed to God, once and even twice. And then I thought I better have enough faith to not pick up that worry again. But something tells me there's a difference between knowing God will take care of it and assuming He will.

There's worry. Time spent with thoughts regarding an uncomfortable circumstance.

There's prayer. Picture the waves on a shoreline – washing in, washing out. Washing in again. And I wonder if our prayer life should be more like that. Staying in tune with God consistently, regardless of the circumstance. Or like breathing; you can't continually breathe in without breathing out. Waves don't come in without going back out. Prayer – state of praying up to God, and a state of settling down. Praying up. Settling down because you know He hears and is concerned.

There's faith. It doesn't mean not thinking about it anymore. But turning your eyes upon Jesus consistently. Time spent with thoughts regarding God's great character and faithfulness. A litany of phrases that you breathe in, and a settling of the heart and mind that comes with breathing out.

Breathe in. Breathe out. Your God hears and is concerned over you. Read through to Exodus 3:16 and see what God promises.

It's going to be a great day!

Everyone was amazed and gave praise to God. They were filled with awe and said, "We have seen remarkable things today" (Luke 5:26).

What makes a good day – *good*? Is it one thing, two things, five things that make the difference? Many consider accomplishment and succeeding good. Others feel it is just experiencing. You desire to lay your head down at night and say, "It's been a good day," but you may be thinking about what more there needs to be done. There is always going to be more that needs to be done. That's called life and living. Some stuff gets done today; some tomorrow. You may wake up in the morning with a list of what you think has to happen today and you rush through trying to get it all accomplished before … before what? Before something else comes along? Guess what … something else is going to come along. Yet you don't have to rush through everything. Some things are meant to sit on a back burner. Some things have a way of working themselves out over the passage of time. Some things are meant to be savored, relished, and appreciated. There is something to be said for steady progression. Fast, immediate, rushing is not always the wisest way. When it comes to what happens in your life today, quality is better than quantity. Seriously consider what went "right" today. Not everything has to be a mile-high mountaintop experience to make it a good day. Stop and think about some of the more simple things in life you are able to enjoy. It doesn't take much to ruin a good day. It can be one or five situations that throw us off from having a good day. But it doesn't

37

need to be viewed that way. Think again about all the good things going on in your "today." Don't let one thing (like the guy that cut you off on your way home) define your day. I'll bet you have a list of goodness already coming to mind. Whether large or small, take time to appreciate and remember the sweetness in life. You have some – every day!

Journal a couple of your own thoughts ...

Holding hands, etc.

Finally, all of you, be like-minded, be sympathetic, love one another, be compassionate and humble (1 Peter 3:8).

May I have permission to say it? You don't know near as much as you think you know about someone's circumstances. I recently visited a friend whose young daughter was in a terrible accident. In that horrific moment, it appeared her life just might be taken from her. And this father's fear was overwhelming with the possible loss. As we talked, his thoughts went back to the Sandy Hook drama. He thought he had felt real compassion on those families that lost children that day. He thought his heart really broke for them. But now, today, now that he's tasted what felt like a close call, he realizes he had no idea the depth of the pain that came from the Sandy Hook shootings and deaths. Whether it's the death of a spouse or news of cancer, it's shockingly different for every one. Don't pretend to know. Even if you've gone through something similar, you don't understand how it has affected *them*. What can you do? You can hold a hand. Cry with them. Hug them. Pray over them. And just sit with them for a bit. Send a card. Make that phone call even when you don't know what to say – just listen. Bring a dinner and stay with them for a while. Remember them long after everyone else has moved on.

The ordinary life

To love Him with all your heart, with all your understanding and with all your strength, and to love your neighbor as yourself is more important than all burnt offerings and sacrifices (Mark 12:33).

One day I stood looking at my reflection in the dresser mirror. And I wondered why God would love a plain and ordinary person like me. Seems like I was just going through life day after day; not making any huge contribution to society.

Then I glanced down and saw pictures on my dresser: one of my mom and one of my grandma. My heart filled with such warmth and love and affection for these two women. And I sensed that they didn't think of themselves as very important or "changing-the-world by storm" people either. But they sure made an impact on me. Without realizing it, they taught me through splashes of love, joy, peace, patience, kindness, goodness, faithfulness, gentleness and self-control (Galatians 5:22). I, too, am a woman of God, living out and passing on the legacy they showed me.

How do you want to be remembered? Show some love, share the joy, grant peace, exhibit patience, extend kindness and goodness, be faithful and gentle, and practice a little self-control. It may not seem as spectacular as more worldly measures of success, but like my "mothers" before me, it will speak volumes. Plain and ordinary indeed! Not in God's eyes. Not by God's standards.

Nurturing a relationship

As a result, Jesus could no longer enter a town openly but stayed outside in lonely places. Yet the people still came to Him from everywhere (Mark 1:45).

I spent a wonderful evening last night. A dozen or so of us girlfriends gathered at a local park. We brown-bagged it. Found a nice place to sit, eat, chat, and look out at the water. We had a good time catching up on each other's lives. We laughed. We shared. We hugged. We prayed. Just nurturing relationships. I was nourished body and soul.

This morning I read a passage in my Bible about a leper who was healed. Jesus warned him not to tell people, but you can see in the Scripture verse printed above, the chapters closing remarks and the results.

O dear Lord, my heart is so saddened after reading that the crowds drove You to lonely places... that the crowds only sought You because they wanted something for themselves from You. They weren't interested in getting to know You, hang out with You, bring joy and helping hands into Your life. They just wanted to be healed of something and then run back to their old life again. How often has my prayer life been about something I wanted fixed or healed for myself? How infrequent are my prayers about getting to know You, hang out with You, bring joy and help into Your life? Your Word tells me all about You; Your created world tells me how beautiful a "Person" You are. More than Savior of my eternity but closer than a

Brother (Proverbs 18:24). You call me Friend (John 15:15). Don't go off to a lonely place. May I welcome You into my day and remember that You are present. May I smile at the very thought of You, Jesus, and bring joy to You instead of always seeking to have You make me feel better. May I be mindful this day of Your company and remember to include You because You are a special, beloved Friend of mine. May I treat You extra special today as I would of any friend coming to visit me. Come, Lord Jesus! Let us spend the day together. It's so good to have You here! Tell me, what have You been up to? Is there anything I can do to help You, my Friend? Let's pray together. Hugs! I love You, Lord!

A free gift for you

The fruit of righteousness will be peace; the effect of righteousness will be quietness and confidence forever (Isaiah 32:17).

A quiet, intimate dinner just for two out on your deck. There's one little candle offering a romantic little glow, soft whispers of few words, a smile, a loving glance your way, watching the sun set and the moon rise, one hand laying hold of another, one star blinks on - and then another.

Pretty plain and simple. Not very flashy at all. It's not like Sunday morning worship at a big mega-church. It's not like a roomful of people celebrating your successful climb up the corporate ladder. It's simplicity wouldn't make most people's top ten list of excitement and accomplishment. Not the most impressive or most expensive place for dinner. Not the biggest name in entertainment. Or is it?

Just a reminder in the midst of all this striving, comparing and measuring in this world that there is a simple beauty in every kind of God-given moment. God can satisfy with the simplest of things. Are you yearning? And even when you strive and strive and arrive, still end up yearning some more?

Perhaps it's time to set your sights on things from above. I know about dreams. And I know that whatever size those dreams are, when God is the Author of them, they come to pass with little or no effort on my part. But in the meantime, while God's timing is unfolding, enjoy the gift of today. Go ahead and dream. Dream big. But don't hang your current happiness on them. Believe God can make things happen. Give your future, your life, your purpose, into His capable hands. Know that He guides the steps to get you where He wants you to be. Believe that He knows the desires of your heart. Believe it is not all up to you to make your future great (and God has His own ideas about what is great – and that's okay). God has a plan for you. A good plan. A part of that plan is to enjoy His gift of today, and rest in His promises regarding your tomorrows. *"For I know the plans I have for you," declares the Lord, "plans to prosper you and not to harm you, plans to give you hope and a future" (Jeremiah 29:11). The fruit of righteousness will be peace; the effect of righteousness will be quietness and confidence forever (Isaiah 32:17). The Lord will indeed give what is good, and our land will yield its harvest (Psalm 85:12).*

An invitation

He makes me lie down in green pastures, He leads me beside quiet waters, He restores my soul (Psalm 23:2).

Jesus invites you, welcomes you, with a gracious smile and a hug into His adventurous plans. He, Who can climb mountains and scale walls and also appreciate green grass and still waters says with a smile, "Come! (You! Yes, you!) Follow Me!"

O dear Lord, I want to follow You. I want to go with You. At least I know that's the best thing to do. But the sinful truth is, I want You to follow me around, and bless what I choose to get into. Forgive my 'I am god' attitude and help me to fear You and acknowledge You as God of the universe. That should be non-negotiable. As in: there is no other truth, no other options. You are in charge. I am not. You set the rules. I follow them. No argument. No discussion. No compromising as though we were equals.

When did trusting and believing (and obeying) become not okay, especially when we're talking about God Almighty?

How in tune are you to the Father's steps these days? If you could be assured of safety and the power to get through anything, would you go with Him today, if you knew truly, with all your heart, that God would be your Strength and your Shield?

A dear friend recently helped me to see Psalm 46:10 in a different light:

BE STILL (stop with all the worrying for one minute!)
AND KNOW THAT I AM GOD.
I AM GOD (not you! I AM GOD Almighty... Creator, Ruler, Lover, and Caretaker of everything in heaven and on earth and under the earth, yesterday, today and forevermore.)

It is safe to follow Him. It is safe to trust Him in what He leads you to do. Isaiah 30:21 assures us, *"Whether you turn to the right or to the left, your ears will hear a voice behind you, saying, 'This is the way; walk in it.'"* Take His hand today. Wherever He leads you, go with God.

I led them with cords of human kindness, with ties of love; I lifted the yoke from their neck and bent down to feed them (Hosea 11:4). My sheep listen to My voice; I know them, and they follow Me. I give them eternal life, and they shall never perish; no one can snatch them out of My hand (John 10:27). He makes me lie down in green pastures, He leads me beside quiet waters, He restores my soul (Psalm 23:2).

Not mundane at all

The King will reply, "Truly I tell you, whatever you did for one of the least of these brothers and sisters of Mine, you did for Me" (Matthew 25:40).

Today is a pretty, drab, ordinary day. I threw some meat and vegetables into the crock pot, mixed up some lemonade and put it in the fridge, cuddled with my two new kitties that we just adopted from the humane society, washed and dried a load of clothes and put them away, did some knitting on a prayer shawl, and sent cards out to shut-ins. Pretty boring stuff, huh? Well, there's another way to look at the mundane and ordinary.

I threw some meat and vegetables into the crock pot *(For I was hungry and you gave me something to eat)*. Mixed up some lemonade and put it in the fridge *(I was thirsty and you gave me something to drink)*. Cuddled with my two new kitties that we just adopted from the humane society *(I was a stranger and you invited me in)*. Washed and dried a load of clothes and put them away *(I needed clothes and you clothed me)*. Did some knitting on a prayer shawl *(I was sick and you looked after me)*. Sent cards out to shut-ins *(I was in prison and you came to visit me)*. Why do we make Jesus' love commands so difficult and complicated? They're not. Take a look at your day and see where you've obeyed. You might just surprise yourself. Little things matter to God. Verse 40 follows up with the following: *"The King will reply, 'Truly I tell you, whatever you did for one of the least of these brothers and sisters of Mine, you did for Me.'"* Your service doesn't necessarily need to be huge and across the other side

47

of the world to be called obedience. You've been called to serve right where you are, too. Your family. Your neighbors. Just day by day following the Lord.

For I was hungry and you gave me something to eat,
I was thirsty and you gave me something to drink,
I was a stranger and you invited me in, I needed clothes and you clothed me,
I was sick and you looked after me,
I was in prison and you came to visit me.
— Matthew 25:35-36

Utterly wonderful

How You made me is amazing and wonderful. I praise You for that. What You have done is wonderful. I know that very well (Psalm 139:4).

I have this vague memory of making caveman furniture with modeling clay and toothpicks under my mom's gentle guidance.

As a small child, I probably started with a snake. Everybody starts rolling out a snake, right? Then I probably twisted the ends together to make a necklace. Not very imaginative, huh? But my mom was pretty creative and she could make something out of next to nothing. That ball of clay would be a coffee cup one minute, a cat the next, and caveman furniture—one thing after another. It was fascinating, entertaining, teaching, and amazing. And one thing was not better than the others. Each thing she made was utterly wonderful to me.

How about you? Are you like clay in God's hands? Do you think He might want to do something new and wonderful with you? Change does not always mean bad. Do you believe that God can shape and mold you from one wonderful thing to another wonderful thing and then to another? Some of us may think we're not so wonderful to start with. That is a lie. God has had His hands on you since before day one. Maybe you're afraid of change. Don't let fears keep you from enjoying a most fascinating, entertaining, amazing time from God. Being molded and remolded doesn't change your basic substance.

I encourage you to submit to molding and shaping in the hands of God and believe everything He makes of you is amazing. Each one is a best; utterly wonderful. Whether a cup or a cat or some furniture, each one has a delightful aspect to it. Enjoy each phase God shapes you to—after all, you are being molded by the Master Creator Himself!

Journal a couple of your own thoughts ...

"God, be _GOD_ for me…"

I will lead them along paths they had not known before. I will guide them on roads they are not familiar with. I will turn the darkness into light as they travel. I will make the rough places smooth. Those are the things I will do. I will not desert my people (Isaiah 42:16).

Come, Lord Jesus … in all Your big, bold, underlined fullness.

I know I'm not supposed to dwell on the past, or my current circumstances, or to plead with God to change what I fear my future circumstances might turn out to be. No matter what, past, present, or future, I need God to be all that He's promised to be: Wonderful Counselor, Almighty God, the Everlasting Father, the Prince of Peace (Isaiah 9:6).

Circumstances certainly do come and go for all of us. Things come to pass (Luke 2:6). And there are times that fully come (Galatians 4:4); at their appointed time (Genesis 18:14). For such a time as this (Esther 4:14).

In all these situations, God, be _GOD_ for me. In all Your fullness.

Wonderful Counselor: help me to acknowledge Your wise presence in my life; that guidance and direction are closer than a whispered prayer.

Almighty God: bigger, better, wiser, stronger than my greatest joy or fear – God of order and reason;

Everlasting Father: with a love that has no beginning or end, no ifs, ands or buts … totally, fully, complete, always caring, parental, nurturing, pursuant love beyond human understanding;

Prince of Peace: a sigh, a release, a rest, security and protection in the present and the future. An absolute. The Peace is here, present. You just need to whisper His Name "Jesus," and you'll sense *something* gentle and soothing … focus on it … it's within your reach … the peace of the living Christ.

Dehydration

Jesus stood and said in a loud voice, "Let anyone who is thirsty come to Me and drink. Whoever believes in Me, as Scripture has said, rivers of living water will flow from within them" (John 7:37-38).

A lot of people coughing and hacking out there, including my poor husband. He said it was hard to cough, because he felt dry in his chest. The doctor said when you feel thirsty, you are already dehydrated. Did you know that? So I put out a couple bowls of water on the heat registers, and do you know what? The water was gone in like a day! Surprised me. Didn't realize our house was dry. So, I've been putting more and more water in as it disappears. I think we both are feeling better. Although I didn't realize we felt bad before.

That's kind of how Jesus, our Living Water, works in us. We can be dry and not even realize it. We can fill up once and not realize we went dry again. And the water in our bowl seems to get used up without us being able to see it happen, just like the bowl I set out. It is a mysterious way of being used for good without actually seeing the living water turn to a vapor. Not a visible steaming boil. But definitely doing something. We see how the living water in us refreshes others, just like the water in the bowl helps me to breathe better and my skin isn't flaking and itching, and there's no electricity in the air that crackles making my hair stand on end.

So how are you feeling today? Dry? Itchy? Crackling with static? Do you even realize what you're lacking? Living Water! Yes, my friend, maybe its time for you to pick up your Bible (again) and have a little tea time chat with Jesus (again). Time to feel better again. Know that He can work in you and through you, (notice I said _HE_ CAN WORK) without you even knowing its happening – like that mysterious vapor. But dry (being without Jesus) is just empty and dry. Don't let yourself get dehydrated.

Journal a couple of your own thoughts ...

Lighter and brighter

He Who was seated on the throne said, "I am making everything new!" Then He said, "Write this down, for these words are trustworthy and true" (Revelation 21:5).

Yesterday was bitter cold. It was kind of dark and gray and snow blowing so hard across the windows, I couldn't see outside. I stayed inside. Air seemed dry and stale in the house, so I put pots of water by the vents. Moved from rocker to sofa ... I was feeling kind of restless; sluggish. Ho hum. Already this winter I feel like I've been stuck inside too much. Cabin fever it's called.

Today, it's still bitter cold. But the sun is shining. Its rays coming through the window, brightening the yellow flowers I have in a vase. I see little birds on the feeder. I went to do a little shoveling. Bundled up, but it didn't feel too awful cold. In fact, it felt kind of good to get out and breathe in some fresh air. And my blood started flowing. I even saw some blue sky. The sun seemed to make everything lighter and brighter. The sun made a difference.

Can the Son do the same thing? Can He make things seem better even when it's "bitterly cold" on the "outside"? With the Son, can you see things that were hidden from your sight before? I'd like to think it is true.

There sure is a difference in my spirit today from yesterday. The only thing that really changed was that the sun came. Instead of thinking about all the things you want changed, how about if we just invite the Son in? Come, Lord Jesus, come! You make all things new!

Journal a couple of your own thoughts ...

Take a walk today

Enoch walked with God... (Genesis 5:24).

Last night, my husband and I walked through the snowy street of the village, side by side, holding hands. We didn't really talk, but I sensed a loving communication between us without the use of words. "I love you," "You are mine," and "I enjoy being with you like this." For a moment, the whole world faded away and it was just the warmth of his hand in mine and the crunch of the snow underfoot and life-giving breath back on my face because of a well-wrapped scarf. Somehow more intimate than just walking side by side.

What does walking with God really mean? "With" means in the company of. "Walking" means moving forward, but not in a hurried manner like running or racing. Steadily moving forward together.

If Enoch was described as this (his life covered in just a couple of sentences in Genesis 5), and this was one of them, it must have been a major part of his lifestyle. Walking with God sounds more intimate, more touchable than having a believing faith for when you can't sense His presence. And yet we are told that He never leaves us. But you must be continually attuned to His presence in order to be described as walking with God. You must acknowledge His ever-presence and converse/connect with Him on some level. He Who is right there ready to listen and lead. It must be a companionable walk, don't you think? A comfortable walk being with Him day in and day out. Strolling side by side, conscious of His presence beyond your morning quiet time. And adoration. Would that be a part of the walk? Love and adoration, a step richer than companionable, comfortable … again, more intimate. Walking with God … I think I like the sound of that. Sounds peaceful. Like on a quiet night street with snow gently swirling, hand in hand, and communicating without words.

Journal a couple of your own thoughts …

You are free

You are free to eat from any tree in the garden, but you must not eat from the tree of the knowledge of good and evil… (Genesis 2:16-17).

Knowledge, hence judgment, was supposed to have been reserved for God alone (knowledge of good and evil). We were supposed to trust God regarding everything. God is a God of peace and order. He meant for us to have abundant life. Relying on Him and not our own knowledge, judgment, and discernment. Total reliance. Total trust. Total belief. Imagine having a peace about every detail being taken care of. Imagine looking to God and being granted direction without the confusion of options. If God knows what is best (and you know He does), and He tells you what is best and He has the best plan for your life, do other choices really matter? Do we really need to experience the power of having all options before us and choosing what we think best from our limited knowledge of the potential outcome? Wouldn't it be easier just to seek the Lord and listen for His voice? You want wisdom? Knowledge? Seek to know the Lord more and more. Read His Word so you know the kind of God He is. That's the only wisdom you need. Know that He never leads you down the wrong path. His desire for you has always been life and blessing. You don't need to eat from the tree of knowledge of good and evil. God has everything you will ever need and He will supply.

God does not want you distracted and burdened and confused with good and evil. He has taken that upon Himself. He alone wants to be the Judge and Discerner. He is a God of peace and order for you. God knows all, and with great love for you shows the way. It is safe to seek Him, hear Him, obey Him, and trust Him. Don't wear yourself out examining all options and possibilities and trying to discern. Too much information is overwhelming, isn't it? And with God at your side, totally unnecessary. You have been set free. It is safe to trust in God with everything. Your reward will be a garden of peace and security and order.

What's abiding with you?

I'm praying not only for them but also for those who will believe in Me because of them and their witness about Me. The goal is for all of them to become one heart and mind – just as You, Father, are in Me and I in You, so they might be one heart and mind with Us (John 17:22).

We've been without power for days. It's inconvenient. It's annoying. It's irritating. What a pain! (Are You there, God? Can You hear me?) And yet, I walked outside to a surreal view of glistening trees with every little branch seemingly seen by the naked eye, sparkling from the street light. And not just one tree, but every tree in every direction. What a breathtaking, beautiful sight! How can such misery and such beauty abide at the same time?

We've been spending our days over at the church. At bedtime, we dash home into the cold house, jump into pajamas and huddle together under a pile of blankets until we get warm enough to fall asleep. (God, can You hear me?) But in the morning, instead of waking up to an alarm clock and getting up and out to hurry into our day, we linger in the warmth of the bed, we snuggle close, whisper and giggle, and doze in and out. What a wonderful thing! There's still no power, but how did such wonderful, memorable moments come alongside such misery as a cold house with no heat?

Are you in some kind of pain? Are there miserable circumstances beyond your control? Look for possibilities of something beautiful running alongside that you have yet to see and experience. We see what we want to see.

Now I'm not saying "every cloud has a silver lining" or "look on the bright side" exactly. But I do believe that pain and pleasure can co-exist and it doesn't have to be all one or the other. If you are suffering, and need a break from it, look for what else might be abiding alongside. Receive respite. What's abiding with you?

Heart and mind

He makes me lie down in green pastures, He leads me beside quiet waters, He refreshes my soul (Psalm 23:2).

I got up again this morning and opened the day with some quiet time prayer. I try to start with just thanking God, for His presence, His generosity and all the other good things about Him. But before too long, my mind drifts to the many on my prayer list: those battling disease, those with financial woes, the grieving, the hurting, the lonely … the list seems so long as one after another come to mind.

I pray inner peace, that despite the circumstances, they see they have a loving Father forging and leading the way through this day.

All your days were written in His book before one of them came to be (Psalm 139:16). Today is no surprise to Him. Certain things have been disallowed to happen while other certain things He saw fit to use for a greater good. Who knows the mind of God? But we know His heart. We know He loves each one of us so much so that He sent His Son here. He Who brought us truths about the *heavenly realm* that we can cling to while we live in the *earthly realm*. Jesus lives with all authority and power, and there is certain hope for believers of eternal life with Him. You get a taste of it whenever you settle down to quiet yourself before Him. After laying your burdens down, that is when you can experience an inexpressible peace inside. You start reminding yourself that God is good, faithful, miraculous and ever-present, and you somehow know you're going to get through this day—even if it's a turbulent one. God will not fail in seeing you through. We don't know how He'll do it (His mind), but we know He will (His heart).

How are you doing today? Set aside all the what-ifs that haven't happened, all the what-ifs about tomorrow too, and take a clear, true look at today. God will see you through. Watch for signs of Him in action. He is here for you today. Breathe. His eye is on the sparrow and I know He keeps an even closer more diligent eye upon you (Matthew 10:31). You name is written on the palm of His hand (Isaiah 49:16). For God so loved you He sent His Son. You will not perish, but have life today (John 3:16).

Sinner and saint

You shall not take vengeance or bear a grudge against any of your people, but you shall love your neighbor as yourself: I AM the Lord (Leviticus 19:18).

Something jogged my memory this morning. I remember having a hard time with a difficult person a while back (quite a while back). And this person was not someone I could walk away from and never talk to again. This person would pop-up into my life on an irregular basis (before you start guessing, most of you do not know this person). Anyway, for me, this person always brought challenges, aggravation and upsets. I had an angry, bitter feeling towards this person. Now how was I going to move past that? This person caused nothing but pain for me.

Then it dawned on me to do a most extraordinary thing. Shift my focus from all the irritants and make a list of the good qualities of this person – even if these good qualities aren't expressed towards me, there could be signs of love towards others. I began writing an actual list. I'll admit it was a struggle at first. I started off with this person really enjoying a certain sport. They are quite creative with some family quality time. They showed devotion to the church. And you know what? My heart started to soften towards this person. Things aren't all bad or all good. There is a mixture of good and bad, saint and sinner, in all of us.

Do you have someone in your circle of influence that is difficult,

65

challenging, tiring, or upsetting? Quietly sit and make a list of the more positive aspects of this person's character. They're there. You just need to shift your focus. It will settle your heart and soul down. You'll be granted more peace, patience, understanding and acceptance. Who wants to be angry and upset if you don't need to be?

Journal a couple of your own thoughts ...

...ALL things are possible

But I say to you, love you enemies and pray for those who persecute you, so that you may be children of your Father in heaven (Matthew 5:44-45).

Remember back to your school days ... some kids were quiet and shy, some fun and friendly, and some bossy and mean. Why was that? I imagine a scenario like this: They woke up having wet the bed, got up late, parents yelling, no breakfast, teased and bullied on the bus, forgot homework, couldn't get locker open ... or imagine a scenario like this: gently awakened by a calm, loving parent, breakfast hot and ready, prayed over as they head out the door, a best friend saving a seat on the bus for them, companionable conversation as they open their locker ... get the picture? Can you imagine how it would affect you? Whether it's a one day thing or endless years – it could be why people act the way they do.

The same could be true of church, or work, or any social club. There is someone rough around the edges. Sharp. Rude. Bossy. Even mean. Why is that? I know you want to turn and run before you say something you shouldn't. But maybe what we need to do is stay and say something you should. Something nice. Put your arm around their shoulders. Give a little pat and a smile. Maybe they don't deserve it, but it could be that they sorely need some gentleness and kindness in their life. And it could just change the direction of the next few moments – instead of escalating or spiraling downward, try to level the emotional direction it could take.

Remember the school kids and do something to make today a little lighter and brighter for someone. Have mercy. Yes, you can. With God, even this is possible.

Journal a couple of your own thoughts ...

Precious you and me

He destined us for adoption as His children through Jesus Christ, according to the good pleasure of His will (Ephesians 1:4-6).

Something precious like a small item set high on a shelf at grandma's house. Maybe it shined. Maybe it sparkled. And at some special moment in time, she took it down and let you hold it. You focused in awe and reverence; taking special care not to mar it in any way (or God-forbid, drop it). Then she'd gently put it back, probably reminiscing some wonderful story behind this special "trinket." Yes, we all know a little something about awe and reverence. Respect. Honor.

The Bible says our bodies are God's dwelling place. Do we really understand that? We picture God far up in heaven, all-seeing, all-knowing – able to reach us to empower us, even way up from His throne on high. We have head knowledge that He is close to us. But the idea of the Holy Spirit within us; Jesus in my heart to stay—is hard to relate with the awe and the hush we might experience stepping into a magnificent cathedral.

Wherever God is - is holy ground. Holy hands, holy lips, holy feet, holy smiles, holy tears—all set apart for God, with holy comings and goings. Having a holy God-honoring countenance all day long. Experiencing awe and reverence for the physical presence—we are an instrument of His peace. Set apart indeed. So be gentle with it.

Handle it with care. Me? Yes, me, along with your fellow believers in Christ. Don't say anything to yourself or to each other that you wouldn't say to Christ. Don't do anything to yourself or to each other that you wouldn't do to Christ. Because we are the Body – the body of Christ. Let's be patient. Let's be gentle and kind with ourselves and others. Love your neighbor as yourself. Turn your thoughts toward awe, honor, respect, and reverence. Your body (and your fellow believer's body) is a temple of the Holy Spirit Who is in you, Whom you have received from God (1 Corinthians 6:19) If you believe the Word to be God-breathed, then believe. It's true of you. It's true of the Christian brother and sister around you. The world can be cold and cruel sometimes. Let's not join its rank when the power of God's love is within us. Today, let's live honoring, respecting and in reverent awe. For the glory of God. You are precious is His sight, and so are they.

Chutes and ladders

Truly I tell you, whatever you did for one of the least of these brothers and sisters of Mine, you did for Me (Matthew 25:40).

My Bible reading today reminds me again of the Holy Spirit power within me (us). There are other spirits out there vying for our attention. But this Spirit, this Holy Spirit, I should be paying more attention to; I should be nurturing that relationship. Too often, I put myself and my mere natural instincts first. It's sometimes hard to tell which spirit I have inside me. I need to start caring about that, and be more concerned about what spirit people see emanating from me. Can I learn to keep being determined to do the godly thing, express godly character instead of natural human reactions? Because I so, so, so-o-o want Christ to be known. Can I somehow make that a determined priority to want Christ to be known? To be known because of the way I'm living my days out.

My first thoughts are, "I won't be able to do it perfectly nor keep it up all the time. I will probably fail 20 minutes from now and I will forget about it 1,000 times today." But if I write it down where I can see it throughout the day, I might remember to do it a few times, and maybe tomorrow a few more times, and that will be more times that the goodness of the Lord will be seen and experienced than had I given up before I even started.

This spiritual journey that we're on isn't a game of chutes and ladders. You don't slide back down with every failed attempt of moving forward. Every time you try to bless others in the character of Jesus, you are moving forward in making Him and His nature known.

So don't you give up thinking godly goodness and kindness in abundance is unattainable. You _are_ capable of reflecting His love over and over again. Because of the Holy Spirit within you.

Me ... worry?

All the days ordained for me were written in Your book before one of them came to be (Psalm 139:6).

I can sometimes be a pretty darn good worrier. Whether it's family or friends or upcoming events, I can spend hours mentally organizing, planning, deciding, list upon list in triplicate with every possible scenario played out in my mind over and over adding more to the "to-do" list. I tell myself I just want to make sure everyone is comfortable, happy, enjoying the good life. Yes, I can be quite the worrier, and quite weary as well.

Sound familiar? Do you sometimes wonder and worry on and on? Does it keep you up all hours of the night? If you are taking on all the responsibility for a successful outcome upon yourself alone, when God is right there, let me remind you of a little something.

God is real, Jesus is alive, and the Holy Spirit resides within you. God has already thought out every detail (even the ones you didn't see coming). When my son went to Iraq, his life was out of my reach; much of it out of my control. But God was here, and there, and seemingly everywhere. The details of those days, I couldn't control; the details I could not even imagine, were all handled by God Himself. He had our backs. He is all-seeing in a good, comforting "thank-God" way. He is all-knowing too. He never leaves you alone. Not ever. It doesn't all depend on you. It doesn't all fall on your shoulders. You have a friend who sticks closer than a brother (Proverbs 18:24).

"Come to Me, all you who are weary and burdened, and I will give you rest" (Matthew 11:28). It's a promise. It's written in blood red ink.

Journal a couple of your own thoughts ...

Common ground, common peace

Let us then pursue what makes for peace and for mutual upbuilding (Romans 14:19).

O dear Lord, help me to understand this day and every day, that everyone is at a different point in their spiritual walk. But we all have the one same God with varying levels of understanding of Him. And they are all just glimpses with no one seeing fully the whole You.

Seek peace and pursue it. First for our own countenance and then for what we can do to bring that peace to others' countenance. We don't need to throw our weight around. We all have different moments when we have a handle on peace and when we don't; greater patience and understanding is what is needed. For there are times when others don't know what you know and that's why they're responding the way they do. And times when *you don't know what they know* and that's why they're responding the way they do. You may think and feel you are in the right, but with more information it's possible your thoughts would be changed. How often have we found ourselves in that exact scenario? We're arguing with someone, trying to impress upon them how right we are and how wrong they are, and then all of a sudden they say something that causes your breath to take a little hitch. "Oh … I didn't know …."

Yeah. You know what I'm talking about. You quickly, quietly back down. So ask God to send up a little flare the next time you become determined to set somebody else straight. Start asking more questions. Gather a little more information and understanding, and be the one to find that common ground that leads to peace.

Let us therefore make every effort to do what leads to peace and to mutual edification (Romans 14:19 NIV).

Journal a couple of your own thoughts ...

Grace? Me?

Then your Father, Who sees what is done in secret, will reward you (Matthew 6:4).

I've been trying to do some Scripture memorization. I started with Matthew 6. I read it over and over and few times, then I try to write it down without looking. I don't spend a lot of time on it. But I do try to be consistent and do it every morning.

It's amazing what can happen.

Right now, the verse above is standing out more than the others.
Now, in this Scripture passage, Jesus is talking about giving and praying, etc. But as my mind wanders and meditates on these words, I see them directing me towards the challenges I face in extending forgiveness to someone when I really want to even the score and pay back. You know what I'm talking about. Someone did you wrong and you want to let them know how un-Christian they were to you. You are angry. You are hurt. And the more you think about it, the more you feel justified in making a mountain out of a molehill. Let go and let God? Really?

Then your Father, Who sees what is done in secret, will reward you (Matthew 6:4).

Forgive. Read a little bit of Romans, Chapter 12. It reminds us not to repay evil with evil. As much as possible, live in peace with everyone. God will deal with the other person and their sins and their spiritual growth.

When I don't react like I want to, when I choose instead to handle it God's way, it feels like I'm doing something good in secret. My heart is really set on pleasing God. God promises to reward.

Journal a couple of your own thoughts ...

Practice, practice, practice

Therefore everyone who hears these words of Mine and puts them into practice is like a wise man who built his house on the rock (Matthew 7:24).

Seems like my memory is not what it used to be. I can handle maybe ten things on my mind at one time. If you give me something more to remember, one of the ten already there gets dropped. I would like to think I could keep everything at a high priority and get it all done, and done well. But the fact of the matter is I must choose what is going to be a priority in my life.

Jesus didn't have much time here on earth. He had to make the most of the time He had. He made choices like: solitary time with His Father, healing the sick, teaching disciples. We, also, don't have as much time here on earth as we'd like to think. This is our one time in history. Are your hands already full? Do you not have any spare moments left? God doesn't call us to add His will to our already full day-planners, but He is asking you to choose your priorities.

And what is God's will for you? I think I'd be safe to say, "Love your neighbor as yourself." We all are strengthened, encouraged, lifted up by a kind thought, word or deed. Let us give evidence of our good principles by good practices.

Formerly, when you did not know God, you were slaves to those who by nature are not gods. But now that you know God - or rather are known by God - how is it that you are turning back to those weak and miserable principles? (Galatians 4:8-9)

We have received Your power in the coming of the Holy Spirit, and we will be Your witnesses (Acts 1:8).

So, today and every day, show some love. Purposefully. Intentionally. Determinedly. Practice extending love, joy, peace, patience, kindness, goodness, faithfulness, gentleness and self-control (Galatians 5:22). Send a card, email, or phone call. How about a hug? Do you have the time?

There are still roses to smell

Then, because so many people were coming and going that they did not even have a chance to eat, He said to them, "Come with Me by yourselves to a quiet place and get some rest" (Mark 6:31).

God has seen us all through some really challenging times, hasn't He? Our parents had some real challenges too, along with our grandparents and theirs. For all kinds of people such as you, me, our loved ones, and strangers, God has been faithful in taking care of all for generations.

Sometimes, life is hard and not just momentarily hard. Pain and fears can set in and linger for days and weeks. But we must choose not to give in to all-day-long, whole life long suffering. Certainly don't deny your feelings. Pray over them. Write down every angry, fearful, frustrated thought. Say it all, then throw it away. Talk with a trusted friend. Face it. Release it. And then stop to take notice of:

- The red cardinal on a black branch with white snowflakes swirling around.
- The aroma of freshly baked cinnamon rolls with frosting running down the sides.
- The mesmerizing dance of a warm fire.
- Roses, to stop and smell.

Because everyone of us, in every generation, at work and school and church, and in every type of neighborhood, no matter how rich or poor, has a life story filled with both joys and sorrows. And God, faithful and true since the beginning of time and through the end of time, will do as He has promised:

To care for the needs of all who mourn in Zion, give them bouquets of roses instead of ashes, messages of joy instead of news of doom, a praising heart instead of a languid spirit (Isaiah 61:3 THE MSG).

Rest in God's faithfulness. Rest in His promises to you.

Twinkle! Little star!

Here's another way to put it: You're here to be light, bringing out the God-colors in the world. God is not a secret to be kept. We're going public with this, as public as a city on a hill. If I make you light-bearers, you don't think I'm going to hide you under a bucket, do you? I'm putting you on a light stand. Now that I've put you there on a hilltop, on a light stand – shine! Keep open house; be generous with your lives. By opening up to others, you'll prompt people to open up with God, this generous Father in heaven (Matthew 5:14 THE MSG).

The other night, my husband and I were traveling along the interstate through mid-Michigan past farms and fields and open spaces. And way off in the distance, I see sparkling lights along a roof line. Farther down the road, there are more twinkling lights. Pretty. Beautiful. Happy. I even saw a house set way back from the road with one little light in every window. Charming. Lovely. Peace and joy come to mind. Even from those one little lights in each window – my, how they shined in the darkness, even from a great distance they had an effect on me.

Can we be a tiny light in someone's life bringing a little loveliness and joy into someone's darkness? Even if they are distant and it's only a little thing we do? 'Tis the season of giving and not just to loved ones here in town. 'Tis the season when Christ's light in us shines most brightly and can reach the most darkest, most unimaginable places. Think of those distant: geographically, relationally, financially, spiritually ... distant (in different situations than ourselves).

John 1: 8 says:

He (John) himself was not the light;
he came only as a witness to the light.
The true light that gives light to every man
was coming into the world.

Make the most of this season, this opportunity to share the light no matter how small the effort, make the effort to touch someone with the light of His love.

Sing … sing a song

The Lord is my strength and my shield; my heart trusts in Him, and He helps me. My heart leaps for joy, and with my song I will praise Him (Psalm 28:7).

Today I want to talk about music (songs and words in a song). We all relate to music … the right song can soothe us, right? Don't you have a favorite song? Is there one that comes to mind when you're feeling blue? Do you hum or whistle a little tune when you're having a good day?

Maybe like a dear loved one of mine, who went through the trauma of having cancer and its treatments, you too, hear a song on the radio and the words speak exactly to what you are feeling. It became her mantra—her strength.

It doesn't have to be Christian music, although those can certainly bring about words of hope and love, encouragement and power. But awhile back, I was listening to a classic rock station, and an old familiar tune came on. The words just washed over me. Not only was I comforted, but a couple of friends came to mind. They have been living busy, harried lives and this song, I knew, would settle them down for a good night's sleep as well. So I simply wrote to them, and said I heard this on the radio and it made me think of them. I jotted a couple lines of the song down and mailed it out.

I have also used choruses of songs to lift up someone's spirits. The old hymns too, have great messages to share, especially to shut-ins. Just a few lines brings hope, reassurance and promise to these dear souls.

And how about an old camp song shared among friends. Revive a good, ol' memory by sending those familiar lines to someone you know.

For those of you who have trouble thinking of something clever or appropriate to write in a card, consider the words written by professional songwriters.

Today, slow down and become aware of the music around you. Listen to the words. Jot some of those phrases down. And then later, take a card and simply write them down and send a meaningful message to someone on your heart. Try it. I've done it. People are blessed by your thoughtfulness.

... and what NOT to say

Jesus wept. The Jews said, "See how (tenderly) He loved him!" (John 11:35-36)

I had a conversation with a dear friend recently. She happens to have suffered a loss of a loved one and also works with others who have. So I feel pretty confident to share some of the things she told me.

Grieving is a terrible business. Grieving is a personal business. Everyone handles it differently. It's mind-numbing. It is life stopping. And it always takes longer than you think.

A few things that just don't help in the time of fresh grief:

- Your loved one isn't in pain anymore. (I don't care! I want my loved one with ME.)
- Your loved one is in a better place. (I don't care! I want my loved one with ME.)
- May you have peace that passes understanding. (I don't want peace. I want my loved one with ME.)
- I know exactly how you feel. (No, you don't. You don't.)

And this next one, used my many of us, innocently and not meaning harm:

- It's been a year now ... it's time for you to move on.

Call it selfish, but the feelings are honest, raw and real. They come in waves – tidal waves. Sometimes they ebb and flow. Eventually, there are days that are better than others. But that empty ache never really goes away. In some ways, you don't get over it in a year or two or ... So, what can we say in these instances? Because we do love and care for this person.

- I am so sorry this has happened to you.
- I am here for you. I'll call you next week. I'll bring dinner.
- I will share your joys and sorrows, 'til we've seen this journey through.

Who do you see?

"Comfort, comfort My people, says, your God. Speak tenderly …" (Isaiah 40:1-2).

I remember writing notes to my brothers who were in the service in Viet Nam. I was pretty young then. Later, I regularly wrote notes to mom, family and friends while I was in the Navy and stationed far from home. And in recent years, my note writing has expanded to shut-ins, friends unemployed, those preparing for surgery, and others suffering through the treatments of cancer. The list goes on. You know them, too. People who are being drained of all the fight left in them. They need a moment of respite. Like a tiny candle in a big, black darkness, a little note from a familiar someone can brighten their day and their journey.

It matters. It makes a difference. With very little effort, you can change the tone of someone's day. Stop and listen to those around you. Pay attention. Every kind and every size of struggle could use some support and understanding. Is there someone facing a big decision? Someone sick and hurting? Facing upcoming surgery? Is there someone trying to stick to a diet? A caregiver being pulled in several directions? A single parent? A loss of a relationship? I have sent cards out in all these cases and I can personally assure you the effort has not been wasted. And I myself have felt better for doing it. It's not about fixing … it's about "I see you and I hear you. You are not alone."

Open your eyes and ears today. Who do you see? And what will you do?

Where is He, indeed?

Your path led through the sea, Your way through the mighty waters, though Your footprints were not seen (Psalm 77:19).

I moved recently. I won't bore you with all the agonizing details of packing, sorting, unpacking, finding places for everything, but there is something I want you to think about and pass on.

I have a ceramic Jesus statue made many years ago by a favorite aunt. Jesus knocking at the door. It's a beautiful piece. A one of a kind piece (my dear aunt is well into her 90's now, and there will be no replacing this treasure). Anyway, during the unpacking and "finding a place for" phase of the move, I looked and looked for the box marked "Jesus".

And I said to myself, "Hmmm … I know He's here somewhere!" And, you know, a little light clicked on inside my head – I KNOW He's here somewhere!

How often we get so focused on the doing or on our current situation, and we do wonder where Jesus is. Your head faith tells you He's here somewhere. May your heart be just as convinced even if you can't see Him, touch Him, or feel Him at the moment.

The benefit of prayer pauses

The Lord is trustworthy in all He promises and faithful in all He does (Psalm 145:13).

My life has gotten increasingly busy lately. I've taken on some projects that are all coming to a head at the same time. I had a hard time falling asleep last night, thinking about all that needs to/should be done. I woke up this morning with the same thoughts, too. I feel so anxious about all that needs to be accomplished and what is most important (and it seemed like a dozen things needed to be done *first!*) But after just a few minutes in prayer, I somehow felt so confident that God would lead me. A peace washed over me. To tell you the truth, I wasn't looking for it, exactly. I was just sitting there telling God how I didn't want to be anxious and overwhelmed, and the next minute, I was "talking" about His character: good, loving, reliable, faithful, powerful, able, wise, all-knowing, and detail-oriented. He knows me, He loves me, hears me, equips me … and when I paused my thoughts after all of that, I realized I was calmer than when I first started praying.

O dear Lord God, help me to remember Your amazing, loving presence and that nothing is going to happen that You didn't already see coming; and that my sins You dealt with long ago on the cross, before they even came to pass. The events of the day ahead have already passed through Your hands. It is safe to move forward because You are already there. I will not get overwhelmed. I will not shut down before I even begin because You, great God, are always with me. I look to You for direction. I look forward to Your guidance in this day. I surrender control, so that *Your power* might be the power really getting things done. May that whole idea fill my head. Anxiety comes from me thinking, envisioning, my feeble abilities trying to accomplish what You've called me to do. Lord, into Your hands I trust You to order my steps in thought, word, and deed.

Pause and let some of that sink in ...Take it to the Lord in prayer. Remember Who God is and what He's done – God never changes. The Lord is faithful to all His promises and loving towards all He has made.

Loving persistence

If you then, though you are evil, know how to give good gifts to your children, how much more will your Father in heaven give good gifts to those who ask Him (Matthew 7:11).

It's been a long time since we've had a baby in the house. But we had a young couple from church over for dinner this past weekend. Their little baby boy was crawling all over the living room. He's going to be up and walking real soon! He kept coming over to the piano bench, trying to pull himself up. He'd get both hands on the bench and one foot planted, but try as he might, he couldn't get that other leg straightened out. I was sitting nearby and would tap a stone coaster on the bench just out of his reach. We were all laughing and smiling and encouraging him, "Come on, baby! You can do it! You're so close! Come on!" Well, he made several attempts that day, but didn't succeed in standing up. He probably got a little stronger and wiser for the next try though. And we all know, he's only a day or two away from victory.

We were lovingly persistent with him. Cheering him on, rejoicing and laughing and celebrating his progress. Do you think that's how God also views our spiritual growth? Can you imagine Him happy and smiling in our attempts, or do you see Him disappointed because you didn't achieve victory right away? Believe me, just as we were loving to that baby boy, God is loving, persistent, and patient with us.

Especially for you

Let us not become weary in doing good, for at the proper time we will reap a harvest if we do not give up (Galatians 6:9).

I remember a friend who suffers from pain everyday telling me a while back, that there are mornings when she really does not want to expend the energy and experience the pain to get out of bed. Then she imagines Satan saying, "Drat! She's up again!" and it's enough to motivate her to take that first step.

Don't ever give up. I understand taking a break. Rest a bit if you need to, but keep your heart and your focus up ahead. Then get back up, brush yourself off, and start again.

Remember a past success, even a long ago success (I won a drawing contest in the sixth grade; a high school teacher used a poem I wrote as a great example to the class). Maybe you didn't pick up a candy bar while in the check-out line (for once!) These are all building blocks to getting you to where you want to be. Don't discount any one of them. Count them up and remember that you have successes in your life.

Rejoice in the steps; don't wait for the final end result to celebrate. My niece loves to celebrate for all kinds of reasons. It makes daily living especially nice. Daily. Living.

Once is not enough

Therefore, everyone who hears these words of Mine and puts them into practice is like a wise man who built his house on the rock (Matthew 7:24).

I recently visited a different church for Sunday morning worship. They sang a song I was unfamiliar with, but I loved the chorus. The first time around, I struggled with the tune/rhythm. The second time around, I listened to the words; the third - finally, really singing the words and making an emotional connection to the words: *Love you so much, Jesus, love you so much.* It sank right into my heart.

It reminded me of reading the same thing over and over again in the Bible. I know that many people put great store in reading the Bible cover to cover. And indeed, that is a good thing. But I've been reading the same chapter (Matthew 6) over and over, and I have to tell you it's been a very educational process. The first few times through, I found a rhythm to what Jesus was saying. Then I pushed myself through the "this is boring," and started really "listening" to the words He spoke with different phrases jumping out at me on different days. Then I started making emotional connections to His words, messages from that passage that would remind me how to respond in life; and the gracious character of God.

I think it's profitable to slow down and really dig in. To try to look at the same thing from different angles, different days, and different moods. And sometimes not be so quick to move on. I think many of us have experienced reading a familiar Bible passage and picking up something "new" we didn't see before. I believe this is God-honoring. I believe it deepens your understanding of God and Who He is. I encourage you to try embracing the Word of God, loving the Word of God, and do not let "Him" go.

Journal a couple of your own thoughts ...

Look for that common thread

Rich and poor have this in common; the Lord is the Maker of them all (Proverbs 22:2).

Whether you're gathered together with some friends on a lazy afternoon, or just sitting around watching the evening news, you can find some hot topics for discussion. Some people think like you do, and some do not. Isn't it aggravating when you can't make someone see things your way? Yet, that is the way of life. No matter where you go, some people will agree passionately with you; others will passionately disagree. It can be as simple as how strong to make coffee. It can be as complex as gay marriage. But the end result is always the same, some people believe as you do and some do not.

Does that mean we keep making divisions in our world, our lives, because there is some disagreement? Do we really want to keep "splintering" our community apart until we're left all alone? Because, I bet we don't perfectly agree on everything with any one person.

Let's be more tolerant of each other, okay? One or two differences in a person does not "ruin" the whole person. That person probably has a dozen other agreeable, wonderful traits. You don't have to like everything about a person. And you can probably find something about a person to like – if you really look (note: the same holds true for yourself – you don't have to like everything about yourself, but there are some agreeable characteristics about you. It's the first step to loving your neighbor as yourself).

I remember a quote from an old Ziggy cartoon: Be nice to people. Not because they deserve it, but because that's the kind of person you are.

Find something to love about the people around you today.

Sticks and stones

And I pray that you, being rooted and established in love, may have power, together with all the Lord's holy people, to grasp how wide and long and high and deep is the love of Christ, and to know this love that surpasses knowledge – that you may be filled to the measure of all the fullness of God (Ephesians 3:17-19).

Many of us are familiar with that old childhood rhyme of sticks and stones, which has the line, "but words can never hurt me." But that's not exactly true, is it? Words can hurt. But I'm willing to bet that often times, those words weren't _meant_ to hurt. Someone either just blurted out a passing thought, or didn't really think through how the message would be received. Whatever the motive, do I get angry, retaliate, tell someone, tell God?

Sometimes, I dwell too long on those words and give them power to ruin my day. Once I think through the hurtful words, and I get past being angry at the other person, and start praying, I am led to confess that I am seeking the love and acceptance of others. I want to be heard by people. Liked by people. When I am hurt by words, it's because people did not acknowledge what I want them to see in me. Too much me, myself, and I? Prayer is always the best way to go.

O dear God, I seek the peace and safety of Your wings. Thank You that You want me to stand up tall and live and that I shouldn't let anyone's comments or words put me in a long-term crouching position. They are just words. Words out of control. The truth of

God's love for me is ramrod firm — a forever staff that supports my standing, upright body.

Words can hurt, but God's Word can overcome, overpower them. Know God's Word. Know His deep, rich, forever faithful love. God is for you. God is on your side. God's love for you is real. God's face shines upon you. God smiles at you. God has your picture in His wallet. God is good.

God hears me. God sees me. God knows my heart and that's enough. It's enough. God understands. God has my back. It's all I need. People don't need to acknowledge my presence or affirm my contributions. God knows. He knows.

I pray for all those who have altered their lifestyle because someone said some hurtful thing. Whether it's not going to church anymore or not eating in the lunch/break room anymore. It's a sad, sad thing when a person isolates themselves because of someone's opinionated words.

There is a way out

No test or temptation that comes your way is beyond the course of what others have had to face. All you need to remember is that God will never let you down; He'll never let you be pushed past your limit; He'll always be there to help you come through it (1 Corinthians 10:13).

Have you been tempted? Whether it's trying to resist a decadent bakery treat or talking yourself out of exercise, or trying to hold your tongue, we all struggle with temptations. And have you struggled even though you prayed for strength? Oh yeah. "Please, please, *please*, Lord, help me not to cave in this time." You <u>plead</u> with God. Yet somehow, it happens. For whatever reason, you do cave in ... ugh.

But sometimes, I don't cave in. I don't let angry words fly out of my mouth. I walk away from the ice cream midnight snack. Because, sometimes, I remember to praise God for how good He is. In my prayer, instead of asking, I remind myself by saying, "God, You are always good. You always hear my prayers. You always care about what's going on in my life. God, You always know what to do. God loves me and I am one of Your wonderful works." God has plans, good plans for my life. God says I am created to be new in Christ so that I can do good things He planned long ago. You recognize some of these biblical truths. In your prayers, start remembering and praising God in these truths and repeat, repeat until you convince yourself these are your truths.

It's hard to remember. It's hard to recall, I know. One thing I started doing several years ago, was to write down on a slip of paper moments when I sensed God really there for me. Times when prayers were answered. Times when I experienced Him and His power turning me away from a temptation. Times in prayer, in worship or in nature when I fully sensed His presence. Then, I slip these pieces of paper randomly in my Bible. Thumbing through my Bible, you'll find all kinds of testimonies of God's great love and provision and sustaining and presence. Remembering Him makes us strong.

Why not? And why not for me?

I have told you these things, that My joy and delight may be in you, and that your joy and gladness may be of full measure and complete and over flowing (John 15:11).

Sometimes we're just too hard on ourselves. Well, aren't we? Don't we take life too seriously and miss out on a lot. Social media was filled with well-wishes this past Father's Day and words of wisdom regarding taking the time to enjoy your kids. Man, they grow up fast! And we waited all winter long for some warm summer days. Now that they're here, are we enjoying them? Like kids, they'll be gone before we know it as well. Now is the time to say, "Why not?" and do something fun and wonderful and totally enjoyable. Don't be distracted by what others might think. For once in your life, say, "I don't care what others think."

Just do it, *because it gives you pleasure.* We all need to take breaks from the worries, demands and full-plates. It's okay to set it all down for a time – trust me, it'll all be right there for you to pick back up again. Take some time to imagine and dream and picture that fun-time you could have on your day-planner. Dream it in full color and detail until you can almost taste it. Then go after it! Go! It's okay to have some fun. It's okay to enjoy your life. You have God's permission to enjoy some abundant life. You <u>need</u> to step away from the daily routine. Sift through the sand. Play badminton. Splash in the water. Toss a Frisbee and make a goofy stretch to try and catch it! Laugh out loud.

Tickle someone. Nuzzle. Blow bubbles. Eat ribs and corn on the cob with your hands. It's summertime! Look forward to something. Get it on your calendar. Something fun. It's good for your health. It's good for your soul. Grab some good! You can make the time. You can.

Journal a couple of your own thoughts ...

Enjoying the view

It was You Who opened up springs and streams; You dried up the ever-flowing rivers. The day is Yours, and Yours also the night; You established the sun and moon. It was You Who set all the boundaries of the earth; You made both summer and winter (Psalm 74:15-17).

Raindrops dripping off the leaves. A chorus of birds calling, chirping, singing. Squirrels in a mad chase across the lawn. A light goes on in a neighbor's kitchen window. The sky slowly lightens as the day begins. Who told the leaves to pop out in glorious full, green foliage in May and not March?

Who caused the ripples in the river to tip at just the right angle as to catch the sun's rays and sparkle like diamonds?

Who cracked open those tiny, hard, little seeds we planted in our garden and now there's green plants making their way through the black dirt?

Who told the robins to look for worms after a rain?

Is it anything less than miraculous?

Whether your view is of a woods full of trees, or sandy lakeside, or a tree-lined neighborhood – even as you look around your own room with your own creature comforts all around you that make it home to you, stop and wonder at the things you call beautiful. How did you end up with such a treasureable sight?

Maybe today's the day you write God a little note.

Journal a couple of your own thoughts ...

Recipe for success

Your word is a lamp for my feet, a light on my path (Psalm 119:105).

I tried a new recipe the other day. I wasn't sure how it was going to turn out. On my own, I'm not much of a cook. So I was a little nervous and doubtful in the beginning that my attempt would look like the picture. With not much experience or knowledge of cooking more complicated dishes like this one, I surrendered to following the recipe step-by-step. I trusted the author of the book. And in the end, much to my surprise, it came out quite good! Woo hoo!

How about you? Have you ever faced something with fear and doubt? Thinking about your own capabilities, strengths, and experience, you can only get so far. May I suggest:

- You look in the "Book"
- You follow step-by-step
- You trust the "Author"

There are endless possibilities beyond yourself with God. Seek Him through His Word and find the recipe to successful living. Despite fear and doubt, put your trust in the Author and follow Him step-by-step. And like me, may you rejoice when it comes out so good!

Taking the leap

So do not fear, for I am with you; do not be dismayed, for I am your God. I will strengthen you and help you; I will uphold you with My righteous right hand (Isaiah 41:10).

I recently saw a picture of a little girl jumping into the big pool for the first time right into her daddy's arms. I remember a similar situation where a little girl jumped from her swing into her daddy's arms. "Stand back, daddy! Farther! Farther!" Kind of scary. But kind of fun too. Safe risk you might say. There are lots of firsts in life. First interview for a job. First big purchase. First time on a plane. Scary, but not unique. Fear of the unknown. Fear of the what-if. But you'll never know if you don't "go there."

Isn't that true of taking any risk? It's about facing your fear of the unknown. But it should also be about moving forward with the "known"—the "known" being the truth about God. *Do not be afraid, I am with you. I am good and mighty and all-wise and all-powerful and all-everything you need.* Isn't that a good description of believing? Facing the fear of the unknown with confidence. Like a daddy catching you when you jump into his arms. A child is certain the daddy can do it, even if they've never jumped like this before. They are sure of the character and the love of the father. You can be to.

Grasping goodness

They rejoice in Your name all day long; they celebrate Your righteousness (Psalm 89:16).

Have you ever had one of those days? Do you know what I'm talking about? By day's end, your spirits are down and you wonder why you ever got out of bed. Was it something somebody said? Or you made a mistake, forgot something ... you fill in the blank.

Did anything good happen on that day? Stop and think. Because many times, we can be guilty of charging a day as "bad," when really only one bad thing happened (okay, maybe two), and we have nursed that bad feeling all day. Do you go to bed listing all the stupid, crummy things that happened?

Well, stop it. With a whole day of the most beautiful, wonderful, amazing things happening all around you, don't you let one harsh word, or one slip up ruin the whole day to the point where you lose your focus on the beauty God brought into your day as well. Yes, there are people with challenging personalities at work, church and social clubs, in the stores and on the road. Don't let them define the memory of your whole day. My, oh my! What a motley crew God has to work with! Shake your head in amazement at what He is able to do through us. And now, imagine yourself enjoying what you have on your daily planner. Imagine yourself having the energy to do it. And all those niggling little worries taking precedence in your mind right now, will you or anyone else remember them 100 years from now? Tonight, when you go to bed, list the things that went right—however small. Small things make a difference in life for you and others. Small things count! Did someone say something negative about you? Well, shame on them. You take a minute right now and say two or three things good about yourself. Come on now, you can do it. You have several good qualities about you because we are all made in the image of God. You extended kindness to someone. You helped or prayed for someone. Good for you!

Have a good day! It's within your grasp.

Live! And in person!

I have made You known to them, and will continue to make You known in order that the love You have for Me may be in them and that I Myself may be in them (John 17:26).

Someone mentioned the other day about sitting at an outdoor café—sun shining, fresh air, fragrant coffee, green trees and plants and flowers and clouds and ... she looked up to see everyone with their nose in their phone. They were missing out on all that beauty!

Which reminded me of times when I've been going down the road and have seen doe and fawns, or turkeys, or some other amazing wonder. And I thought about people who have missed out on that unexpected beauty because they were texting on their phone instead being in the present and enjoying all that is around them.

Which led me to think about the days long ago when I took little ones to the zoo. Always a controversy about having wild animals caged up like that. But seriously, without a zoo, many children would never see a Siberian tiger or polar bear or peacock. Without an effort being made to bring the live animals to them, they would only know a small, still photo, or animated version of the real thing.

Which then led me to consider the ways we need to bring Jesus to our world. _Alive_. If we only hand people a book, a photo, even animation, or snippets of Bible verses – it all falls so short of the "real thing." You've heard all the familiar expressions before: Jesus with skin on, or, the hands and feet of Jesus. Remember the story in Acts 8 about Philip and the Ethiopian? "How can I (understand) unless someone (takes the time to) explain it to me?" I'll bet you can think of someone right now who needs to feel the living, present love of Jesus. A hug. A smile. A little one-on-one conversation. A little hand holding. We sing it at Easter time ... Jesus is alive! Let's make an effort to live it out for someone today.

Comfort, comfort my people

As a mother comforts her child, so will I comfort you (Isaiah 66:13).

When I first hear the word "comforter," I think of the "blanket" I like to snuggle up with when I'm feeling poorly – physically or emotionally. Yeah, like a little kid … all warm and cozy. Comfortable. Safe. A place where you can just <u>BE</u>. You don't have to be happy-go-lucky. You just snuggle down and can even pull the blanket over your head. It's acceptable. The sign is out: I'm not feeling good.

There's another use of the word "comforter" that really isn't that much different. I was with a small group of trusted friends, and shared something I was challenged by, struggling with, troubled about, and I looked around and saw several heads nodding in agreement. And they had insightful comments. They could relate. They knew what I was experiencing. They had been there. They were beside me. I was being heard. And understood. What a beautiful, beautiful gift. Not feeling "good" and still being accepted. Safe.

You'd be hard-pressed nowadays to find someone whose life has not been touched by the trauma of cancer. But back in the early days of its discovery, imagine the fear and the loneliness of having to experience that without someone else coming along side and saying "I know…" And even when you aren't quite sure what to say, it is very supportive to reflect back the emotion you hear in that person's voice: "You sound frustrated," "It sounds like a very anxious time," or "You sound tired of all the added pressure." Whether it's a small group discussion, or an AA meeting, or a cancer support group, or mothers of toddlers group, or a grief support ... there is *comfort* in knowing someone else has suffered as you are now and understands. We often wonder why we have to suffer. Well, just think of a time when you were suffering and found someone nodding their head in compassion and understanding. What a beautiful, beautiful gift, right? Paul, in the second letter to the Corinthians tells us about God being the God of all comfort, who comforts us in all our troubles, so that we can comfort those in any trouble with the comfort we ourselves have received from God (2 Corinthians1:3-4). I wrote a note to myself in the margin of my Bible: If you don't need big, and don't ask big, then you don't need divine intervention. God is still the answer. And we comfort those in any trouble with the comfort we ourselves have received from God.

Determining value

This is the day which the Lord hath made; we will rejoice and be glad in it (Psalm 118:24).

One day…

I got up early and skimmed through the day's one-page devotional, gulping down a cup of coffee before running off to a weight management class, then heading over to the gym, after stopping for gas. Then I met someone over at the church to help do an inventory in the kitchen. I went back home to start a couple loads of laundry. I got that all washed, dried, and put away. I then grabbed a bite of lunch while preparing the agenda for an afternoon meeting. Continuing, I made copies, led that meeting which morphed into a sub-committee meeting, watered my flowers, filled the birdfeeders, ran to the store for some items necessary to prepare dinner, swung by the post office, wove in and out of traffic like a pro, cooked dinner, prepped and picked up for an evening discussion group held at our house, and updated the calendar with more upcoming family events.

One day…

I laid around in bed an extra long time listening to the morning rain, and then lingered over a cup of coffee as I watched the sun rise from my side porch and communed with God while I read from my Bible. I rambled on leisurely to God as my thoughts and dreams were written in my journal. I did a little sketching and a lot of smiling. I wrote out a few notes to some dear friends I miss very much and haven't seen in forever. I strolled down to the post office, praying for my neighbors along the way, appreciating His beauty in the flowers and the river and the kids riding their bikes. I enjoyed a bowl of cantaloupe – fresh and clean and juicy. I listened to my favorite music and sipped a splash of wine while I prepared dinner. I hugged and kissed my husband when he came home. We chatted casually, unhurriedly. We snuggled together on the couch while the day came to its close.

In a world where value is measured by activity and production and to-do lists, let us not be confused. While all these things are good, don't be mistaken or misled – there is value in contemplative, appreciative, slower pace days. So I say, slow down and enjoy your life today.

Living a fruit-filled day

Because of the Lord's great love we are not consumed, for His compassions never fail. They are new every morning; great is Your faithfulness (Lamentations 3:22-23)

I hope you were able to enjoy a beautiful warm spring day yesterday. It turned out to be a great one for me. Not only did I make it to the gym first thing in the morning, I made healthy food choices all day, and my husband and I spent some time in the afternoon working on outdoor projects together. We scraped bubbled up paint from the deck. We started clearing out a long lost garden over by the garage. We sat under the pine tree and enjoyed a cooling breeze and icy drinks. Plus dinner out later on!

This morning when I was thanking God for all that blessed time, this thought ran through my mind:

LOVE – Lord, I love my husband

JOY – simply being outdoors and working together on a project

PEACE – sitting together under the pine tree enjoying the sight of what we got accomplished

PATIENCE – appreciation of what got done without having to have it all completed right away

KINDNESS – getting refills on our ice cold drinks

GOODNESS – working in the black soil, warm sunshine, cool breeze, good company

FAITHFULNESS – God's presence; sticking to healthier lifestyle choices

GENTLENESS – considering my words ... words of support and encouragement vs. any criticism as we worked together

SELF CONTROL – did not consume my whole dinner but brought some home

Wow! I hadn't considered before how my day could actually be filled with the fruit of the Spirit. How about you? Or maybe you have a loved one near to your heart that could use this insight as well.

God, are You there?

Your path led through the sea, Your way through the mighty waters, though Your footprints were not seen (Psalm 77:19).

Several years ago, I got up in front of a roomful of people for my very first public speaking engagement. You know with a podium and a microphone and everything! Yes, shy, introverted *me*. I was scared to death. I think my list of "what-if's" was longer than the actually speech itself. I worked and worked and practiced and prayed over that speech for a long time. I told myself a thousand times that I trusted in God to come and rescue me from all my fears. But I still felt shaky and nervous. I even had a friend pray over me right before I stepped out to the podium. But I still had knees knocking, hands shaking, eyes popping, and heart pounding anxiety even after all this prayer...

"God? God, I thought You promised to help me in times of trial? Why am I still so afraid? Don't I trust You enough?"

Well, I made it through my presentation. Some wise person told me to write on my notes things like: smile, pause, look up and out, etc. And I think I unconsciously followed through on all my notes. I made it through and people said I did just fine. I went up and made my presentation despite the fact that I couldn't sense God's presence in the "what-if" moments beforehand. My head and my heart still believed in Him.

How about you? Do you have a "what-if" event coming up? It doesn't have to be public speaking. Is there some worrisome thing unfolding, perhaps with a loved one, and you fear the outcome? And you're not feeling 100 percent peace – even though you pray – the anxious thoughts keep niggling…

Trust in the Lord with all your heart and lean not on your own understanding. In all your ways acknowledge Him, and He will direct your paths (Proverbs 3:5).

Surely not I, Lord

... to equip His people for works of service, so that the body of Christ may be built up (Ephesians 4:12).

I'm going to make myself a little vulnerable here, and maybe somebody else as well. Because something happened Sunday morning. And no matter how scary, risky it can sometimes be to share a God moment, they should be shared. Because we all need to see God alive and well and working in our present day lives.

I walked into church Sunday morning. After a five-day sabbatical retreat, where God indeed spoke some encouragement to me. So, I'm at church early and someone mentions to me that an unfamiliar face was sitting in the sanctuary off to the left. (I guess they tell me these things because I'm the pastor's wife and I should be aware). Now, those of you who know me, *know* that I am way too shy and introvert to actually walk up to a stranger and start talking. But I bravely walked down the center aisle and turned to the *right* to start a conversation with the choir director's wife. (Safe!) But I was still drawn to the "stranger." Ugh. My feelings say don't do it, way out of my comfort zone, but somewhere in my heart I know talking to this "stranger" is the right thing to do. Somehow, and I truly mean somehow I walk over and sit down and talk to this woman. I have no idea how to start a conversation, or carry on a conversation with a stranger. My feelings are worried about ME. But the Jesus in my heart is worried about *HER* and Jesus won out. I sat and talked with her. I helped her through the bulletin. I helped her find the hymns, the Scriptures, the Apostles Creed, and handed her a tissue when she silently cried. I was blessed when I heard her whisper, "Yes!" and "Oh, wow!" as the pastor explained a gospel lesson I had heard many times. I heard the miracle in the Scripture story through new ears giving me fresh insight and appreciation. Now I admit, there were moments (before the service started) when I tried to ease myself away, but something held me there. And by the grace of God, the right thing to do happened. Obedience paid off in blessing for the both of us. Praise God for His "something-somehow" power.

And I wept…

You keep track of all my sorrows. You have collected all my tears in Your bottle. You have recorded each one in Your book (Psalm 56:8).

Sometimes crying just makes us feel better by providing some sort of release for a built-up energy inside. And sometimes tears just burst out and seem to have no end.

My beloved mom seemed like a pretty emotionally strong person. As a kid, I didn't see her cry often. But at her mom's funeral, she wept aloud and she wept hard; I don't think anything broke my heart more. That is, until my own mom died. Then I never wept so uncontrollably in my whole life. Such overwhelming sadness! Such personal loss.

Why am I bringing up such dark, painful memories now, especially when beautiful spring weather and Easter Sunday are right around the corner? Because today is Maundy Thursday. All these gray Lenten days are culminating in a truth that my heart can hardly bear:

Jesus *died* …

I look back over my life and realize how lost and far from God I was. No promise of a beautiful life in heaven on my own merit. No hope at all. Separated from the God of all possibilities.

There's a passage in Revelation, Chapter 5, where after describing this incredible, beyond human imagination scene unfolding before his eyes, John then hears a booming voice shout:

"Who is worthy to break the seal and open the scroll?" (Revelation 5:2)

John's response? Read the first line of verse 4:
I wept and wept because no one was found who was worthy to open the scroll or look inside.

And I ask you to pause there for a moment. Conjure up a memory of a time when you wept and wept, because it felt like there was no hope in overcoming some tremendous, heartbreaking, emotional pain you were experiencing, and then ponder this deep truth:

Jesus *died* ... *for you.*
(read each word slowly)

And now, the good news. Continue reading verse 4:

Then one of the elders said to me, "Do not weep! See, the Lion of the tribe of Judah, the Root of David, has triumphed. He is able...
He is able...

Rain, rain go away

Finally, brothers and sisters, whatever is true, whatever is noble, whatever is right, whatever is pure, whatever is lovely, whatever is admirable — if anything is excellent or praiseworthy — think about such things (Philippians 4:8).

Another gray sky, brown grass day. Hmmph. I waited every day last week for some beautiful, spring-like, renewing "something" to happen so that I could post to my blog a refreshing, inspirational message. But I had one ordinary day after another. And here it is, the beginning of a new week and it's starting off as another gray-brown day.

I guess it can be said of all of us. We want everyone to see us at our very best. Sunny and bright and hopeful and encouraging and light-hearted. But that's not real life, is it? The truth is: in between the highs and lows, there are some pretty ordinary "blah" days — blah perhaps because we have such high expectations.

But life is constantly moving forward. The highs don't last, the lows don't stick around forever (good thing to remember); and these blah end of winter days won't be here much longer either. Life is constantly cycling through. If there's one thing you can count on, things are going to change.

I think I'm going to spend a little time creating my own refreshing moments. Someone posted on social media the other day a saying something about I'm tired of being an adult. I'm going to hide in my blanket tent and color! And it got me to thinking about some pure, innocent, childhood fun. What was your favorite childhood toy? (paper dolls) What was your favorite childhood game? (hmmm ... hopscotch) What was the best movie you ever saw as a child? (Ol' Yeller) What about favorite childhood food? (of course, it's ice cream with banana cut up on it with chocolate syrup!) Goodness, I'm feeling better already! Sitting here writing all this down has taken my focus off the gray brown outside. Could there be a lesson there? Take your eyes (and your thoughts) off the circumstance and turn to something sweet and wonderful. Whatever is lovely, think upon these things. (Philippians 4:8) Apply biblical principles (truth) to your day today.

Crazy love

Satisfy us in the morning with Your unfailing love, that we may sing for joy and be glad all our days (Psalm 90:14).

I have value and worth, because it is God Himself Who created me. By His good plan and purpose, He put me here in this place and time. God, Who loves me like crazy all day and night … Who is always with me, watching over me, and always caring about me. Blessing me with good gifts. It is true! He never stops being crazy in love over me. He loves and understands my crabby days. Bad hair days. Backsliding days. Fearful days. Acts of kindness days too. Regardless, His love for me never changes. It's always at its biggest, brightest, greatest, broadest. He loved me before I ever committed a sin and He loved me before I ever did any good works. He cannot love me more and He will not love me less. Grasp the extravagant dimensions of Christ's love. *We no longer believe just because of what you said; now we have heard for ourselves, and we know that this Man really is the Savior of the world (John 4:39-42). Satisfy us in the morning with your unfailing love, that we may sing for joy and be glad all our days (Psalm 90:14).*

By God's measureless grace, you are loved no matter what, and you are valued no matter what. Separate from your career accomplishments (or lack thereof), financial success (or lack thereof), motherhood/fatherhood (or lack thereof), marriage (or lack thereof) – you are loved and valued in all the past and present things. God, GOD, **GOD!** genuinely, tenderly loves you. Like a newborn baby …

yeah, like that. God loves you greatly … all the time. *His banner over me is love (Song of Solomon 2:5). The Lord your God is with you, the Mighty Warrior Who saves. He will take great delight in you; in His love He will no longer rebuke you, but will rejoice over you with singing (Zephaniah 3:16-18).* And don't forget: *For God so loved … (John 3:16)*

Journal a couple of your own thoughts …

Pleased with ordinary things

... the unfailing beauty of a gentle and quiet spirit, which is of great worth in God's sight (1 Peter 3:4).

Maybe it's the cold, gray, February weather. Maybe it's me finally getting used to not having to go to work every day. Instead, I have the whole day available to do whatever. But either way, I feel myself getting a little restless or bored, or not living very usefully or purposefully.

So in my morning prayers today, I asked God, "Who am I and why am I here? What should I be doing? What is my purpose for being here in this place and having all this 'free time?'" Some worthy activity ... some passionate purpose ...

No response from God. Stillness. Absolute quiet. Nothing. Not one word from God.

Have you been there? Desperately seeking God and no sense of response from Him?

I finally decided to knit and rock here in my chair for awhile. And picked up the prayer shawl I've working on. Yes, you read that right – *a prayer shawl*. As in, making something for the benefit of someone else, and praying along each row for someone's health and well-being.

To have it ready and available for a fellow church member in need. BAM! Answered prayer. Some worthy activity!

The more I thought about this startling, immediate, answered prayer, the more excited I got and the more energized and passionate I became about writing about it and sharing it with others on my blog. BAM! Answered prayer. Some passionate purpose!

Praise God! Answered prayer can happen just like that! (snap your fingers)

1 Peter, chapter 3 says that God is pleased with gentle, quiet things.
2 Timothy, chapter 2 says that some purposes are noble and some ignoble … an instrument made holy, useful to the Master and prepared to do any good work.

2 Corinthians, chapter 4 says we are jars of clay. It's easy to forget that we are the packaging and His work is the treasure.

Yes, I believe He is pleased with small, ordinary things, things that carry the love of God. So, what small thing can you do for someone today?

.

Like ... "a lot"

Therefore encourage one another and build each other up, just as in fact you are doing (1 Thessalonians 5:11).

So many of us, at least once (if not more) in a day, scroll through our favorite social network. I did again this morning. Everyday I see: funny cartoons, support for various causes, pictures of family and friends near and far, prayer requests, happy couples, happy friends, happy children, happy dogs, sadness, hurt, loss, broken hearts, too, vacation photos, the weather, upcoming events, and lots of "likes".

The mixture of ups and downs is always the same, a mixture of good and bad, happy and sad. But the face of those posting seems to rotate and take its turn. We all get a dose of these various life happenings. So, maybe it's not so bad that we share, because at some point we experience it all. It sure is encouraging when someone "likes" what you wrote. It sure is comforting when many comment "they will be praying." It's heart-warming to "see" friends I haven't seen in a long while; heart-warming to see my son's smiling face. Good to be aware of various health issues and causes. Good to join in. Good to not feel alone in something.

It just struck me this morning, what a great, big world we live in. What a great number of folks are out there ... all living and feeling and experiencing days and nights and life, just as I am. And how coming alongside through a simple "like" or "comment" can make all the difference in the world. "Like" can bring renewed strength and hope.

I believe people want to be known. People want to be heard. Whether they express sadness, fear or joy—to have someone come alongside and say, "I see you. I hear you. I will remember you while you are going through this." There is an awesome power at work when we feel remembered. It says, "I have time for you. You have value." Wow!

So, whether it's a card or a phone call or a simple "like," let's stick together. Let's encourage and support each other in this journey. And let's do it often.

Refreshing freedom

God rested on the seventh day (Genesis 2:2).
Jesus often went off to a solitary place (Matthew 14:23).

Even the earth, creation, seems to rest for a season.

We work hard to follow their examples when it comes to "doing," but somehow feel guilty when it comes to following their examples of resting.

Date night with the spouse, but you constantly worry about the kids with the babysitter. Taking a day or two (or more) off work and constantly worrying about the mess piling up on your desk. An illness which has you home-bound or bedridden for a time. And retirement, you get to live your life not strapped to someone's timeclock, yet some people feel guilty for not having every day - jam-packed days. Saying "no" to a committee you have served on several terms already. Or simply laying in bed "longer than you should."

Why do we feel so guilty about resting? *Because we see it as doing nothing.* What does **REST** really mean? Here are a few of the definitions I found in the dictionary. See what they bring to your mind:

- A state or period of refreshing freedom from exertion.
- The repose of sleep that is refreshing to body and mind and is marked by a reduction in metabolic activity.
- Something used for support.

- To allow a person or animal to regain energy by means of relaxation or sleep, or allow a limb or body part to be inactive to restore its strength.

- Refreshing freedom ... support ... regain energy and strength.

A time of rest sounds like a necessary thing in order to continue on with one's life and living. Sounds essential. So let's stop feeling guilty when we take time to rest in between all the doing. Whether it's a ten-minute break from your desk or a week away, God is in the business of restoration while you are doing "nothing."

Who will I be today?

Christ gives me the strength to face anything (Philippians 4:13).

I got a bracelet as a Christmas gift. It says: "Dreams become reality one choice at a time." The local restaurant owner here, when asked what his plans are for the future, said: "I plan on being here tomorrow." And on a website for healthier living, I found listed: "Envision what it will feel like." Aren't we all guilty of making something look incredible difficult, impossible? Do we bite off more than we can chew (no diet pun intended), before we even start? Whether its dieting, or reading the Bible straight through, or considering a new hobby, a new job, organizing the home office, straightening up the basement, getting to the gym, even having good intentions to send more cards out this year ... do you wish you were more (_____ fill in the blank), but just can't seem to get the ball rolling and keep it rolling?

(I'll fill in the blank) I want to be someone who is more organized. I want to be someone who has a healthy attitude about diet and exercise. I want to be someone who shows love and compassion towards others.

It feels impossible to give up bread and sweets completely and forever so that I can lose weight, right? That basement is filled, filled, filled with boxes ... all of them half-opened and dug through; it will take forever and a day to get it all organized. Changing clothes to go to the gym, driving to and from in this weather, re-showering … every day for the rest of my life. Do you see where I'm going with this? We need doable, bite-sizes of change/ improvements.

I'm going to take the advice from the bracelet and make it happen one choice at a time.

I'm going to take the words from the restaurant owner and make plans for one day at a time.

I'm going to take the advice from the website and imagine myself, just for today, as someone who will do at least one thing as the person I desire to be.

So that, at the end of _this_ day, I can say to myself,
"I was helpful today in encouraging others to have hope, because I wrote a blog post."
(I am a HELPFUL kind of person)
"I was thoughtful today because I mailed out a thinking of you card."
(I am a THOUGHTFUL kind of person)
"I was kind today because I helped someone brush the snow off their car."
(I am a KIND kind of person)
How about you? Just for today, what kind of person will you be?

Going the wrong way

Trust in the Lord with all thine heart; and lean not unto thine own understanding. In all thy ways acknowledge Him, and He shall direct thy paths (Proverbs 3:5-6).

I can't begin to tell you how many times I get lost driving myself somewhere. It is to the point of being embarrassingly ridiculous. There have been times I've had to pull over because I was crying so hard – lost and scared. I'm late. People are waiting for me.

So after suffering through this dilemma numerous times, it was no surprise to me that I got lost going to a friend's house yesterday. She was supposed to be only an hour away! I had the directions clearly written out on a piece of paper. But an accident on the highway sent me off on a different exit than the one I needed and **off** I surely was! A quick phone call to my friend and it sounded like a couple turns here and there and I'd be right back on track. I don't know how it happens. It certainly seemed clear to me at first. But like the other times, I'm going down the road looking for a certain landmark and it never shows! So I make a couple turns that I think make sense. But I was sadly mistaken. There I am. On the corner of Clueless and Hopeless.

I tried hard not to focus on the potential calamity. Instead I just kept saying, "Lord, I am trusting You. Lord, I am trusting You." I'll admit, there was a moment or two beyond just "oh, good grief!" when I really started wondering how long it would take me to find a way back to something familiar. But I kept thinking about the faithfulness of the Lord. And then quite suddenly I found myself on a corner of a main road and there was a mail truck nearby. I'll just ask for some direction! Then I looked up at the road sign and it had the name of the street I was looking for all along! True story. I was just a few miles too far south of my destination.

Where are you headed? Do you have clear direction? Do you stop and ask for help along the way? Or do you think you know what to do on your own? Are you on the corner of Clueless and Hopeless? Are you a little south of where you're supposed to be? Do you panic or do you trust in God?

Pass it on!

Share with the Lord's people who are in need (Romans 12:13).

Ever read a daily devotional and nothing jumps out at you? Yeah. Or when you read the Bible, you "come up dry" and get a "thirst for a special message just right for me" feeling … just right for my own special need or situation. Hmmm… sitting there. Wondering. Praying for meaning. A thought about a friend comes to mind. I push it aside. This is *my* quiet time with God. *My* time to be fed and directed by Him, so that I know how He wants me to follow Him today. Friend comes to mind again. And yet again. I look down at what I was reading. A phrase. A verse. The friend again.

Could it be that the message I am seeking is not for me at all, but for a dear friend? God is directing me to be a conduit; a messenger. He's wanting me to pass something on.

Coming up empty after reading a devotional or Scripture? Ask God if He has someone else in mind, and pass it on!

Will you come and follow Me?

Therefore if you have any encouragement from being united with Christ, if any comfort from His love, if any common sharing in the Spirit, if any tenderness and compassion, then make my joy complete by being like-minded, having the same love, being one in spirit and of one mind (Philippians 2:1-2).

This recent media frenzy over "ice bucket challenge" for ALS certainly has caused a lot of attention. Somewhere, somehow, someone got stirred deep within their heart about this disease and got so caught up and passionate about it that they had to do something. And something they did!

There are numerous causes out there. We can feel compassion towards each one as we are made aware of the pain and suffering they each cause. But we don't have the time, energy or resources to be passionate about all of them. No, I think God places in each one of our hearts a certain passion. It is a nagging thing that just won't let go. Whether it's unfair treatment of vets or senior citizens, or a debilitating childhood disease, there will be certain things that make our heart really ache.

I am currently working on writing a "speech" on Laity in the Church for an upcoming spiritual retreat. And I am reminded that God may be working in the same way in our churches. Are there certain aspects of the church life that you are passionate about? Things that you see should be done in the utmost way? Do you think, talk, dwell and imagine how it should or could be? Don't ignore God's calling. He may be making your heart break over something that is also important to Him. Laity is not somebody else in the church. Laity is you. And you were meant to be with God in the on-going nurturing of the church's health and well-being. God's kingdom plan includes you. Yes, you! An avid golfer eats, drinks, sleeps, dreams, talks, writes, reads – GOLF. I'll bet if you thought about it, there is something about church life that could consume you into action as well. Like the golfer or the creator of "ice bucket challenge," you could be a conduit to God's great passion for something in your church. Wouldn't it be exciting to birth something new? God can do that. He just needs open hands ready to carry the work He already has in mind. What does God love that He wants you to love just as passionately? Do you feel the nudge? Will you follow Him?

The power of five

And let us consider how we may spur one another on toward love and good deeds (Hebrews 10:24).

I like ordinary days. Days where there are things planned to do, but not too many things. Nothing stressful in view. Time for doing what I want. I had a day like that today. Didn't really expect anything. But God is full of surprises.

I received a lovely little note from a friend today. A real snail mail note. It contained five sentences. Yes, five. Full of love and encouragement and it touched my heart in such a deep way. A little note? Five sentences? Yes. It lifted my ho-hum spirit into a whole new, exciting, glad-to-be-alive kind of feeling. I moved from content to happy. I read it over a couple of times and it brought warm, fuzzy feelings about this friend to mind. And I wanted to reach out and touch her with love right back!

Don't underestimate the power of your words. Even a few words. Who doesn't need a little encouragement and love – ever! Any day is a good day to pen a line to someone in your sphere of influence. I would love to suggest to all of you to keep a pack of note cards handy. There is a serious power at work there. Power to uplift. She turned my day from ordinary to extraordinary with a minute or two of thoughtful writing.

I love this friend. I know when her husband died, a piece of her died with him. But I am so grateful to God that there remains a part of her still loving and living in my life. Can you think of five sentences of kindness? Can you be that friend to someone today? Living as a Christian in this world is hard. Let us spur one another on!

Journal a couple of your own thoughts ...

Oh Lord, hear my prayer

God has surely listened and has heard my prayer (Psalm 66:19).

I have some friends who are at the end of the rope. Have tugged and choked and squeezed out all the faith they have, and still trying to trust in God despite the agony of the situation. Physical pain has a way of getting our full attention. They have prayed and prayed and tried to do everything they've been told to do. Still ... the pain.

It's hard to connect with people in this situation. It's hard to know what to say for we surely don't have any good answers either. I mean, if the doctors don't know ...

But we have a Brother, Who knows the depth of such pain. Ongoing, strangling pain. And I'm not sure that His knowing His pain was for a good cause helped Him in the midst of the actual minute after agonizing minute of hanging by nails on a cross. We know He suffered unimaginable pain. We know people who have to do the same. Like Him, they have to bear it.

This is where prayer is so desperately needed. Because pain can clog your brain, causing you to focus not on what you know and believe. It's the ultimate distraction. And can render a person helpless in praying to God for healing and comfort.

WE NEED TO PRAY. We need to be the ones to carry the burden

to the Lord on their behalf. Please do it. Please pray for someone today. They have run out of words. They are becoming shaken and losing their grip. Your prayer does indeed stand in the gap for someone. God hears you. God listens. God cares.

Journal a couple of your own thoughts ...

Putting it down

Come over here, my friend, and sit down (Ruth 4:1).

The cooler weather brings out the "knitting bug" in me. In the past, I have entertained myself by working on mittens of every size and color. I had found a pattern that was easy enough, but this year I decided to stretch myself and try a whole sweater. After scouring the stores to find just the right yarn, I was ready and excited to dive in and get started.

Knitting can be both relaxing and exhilarating. The more you get done, the cooler it is, which makes it really hard to put your project down. Such was the case the other day. I was happily knitting along, rocking in my chair and humming, when a big clump of yarn bumped my hand. I tried pushing it farther down the line, but it quickly came up against my hand again. I tried pulling more yarn out of the clump. Only a few inches were gained. Grrr! And the clump seemed to be getting both bigger and tighter. A mess! Things were going along just fine, and now this horrible knot is the only thing I can see. I finally set both my needles down, and with my other hand pulled the string of yarn from the opposite end. With some slow and easy pulling and a gentle shake or two from this other hand, the knotty mess loosened and broke apart so I could continue on my way.

Ever have days like that? Frustrating problems at home or work? Struggling on your own only seemed to make things worse. Then a friend with a helping hand comes along and opens your eyes to a different angle, and viola! What a friend! The situation had been diffused … crisis diverted. And you're moving again.

Now, can you be that kind of helpful friend? And how? Sometimes, people just need to be reminded to put their work down, to stop or slow down, take a deep breath, or walk away and come back later. A few soothing words can go a long way. They may need a diversion. A respite from the trial. An intermission for hope.

Refocus

When He came near the place where the road goes down the Mount of Olives, the whole crowd of disciples began joyfully to praise God in loud voices for all the miracles they had seen (Luke 19:37).

It certainly isn't hard these days to find bad news; heart-breaking news. It seems all too easy to make a list of things to worry about, lose hope about. Do you have a list of circumstances in your life where getting things turned around seems impossible? Waiting and waiting and things aren't appearing to get all better. I believe bad news and good news run alongside each other, like railroad tracks.

For some reason, bad news seems to jump out at us, screaming for attention, and attention it gets. Good news on the other hand, is just as present, but you have to "force yourself" to acknowledge its presence. Because good news IS present. So let's practice refocusing.

I want you to stop and think for a minute of how many cancer survivors you can name. Make a list.
And how about those who have survived serious surgeries … add them to your list.
Do you know some who made it through a life-threatening accident?
How many people do you know who were unemployed and finally got a job?
A soldier home from the war…
A complicated pregnancy - had a healthy baby…

Someone returning to the faith…

A couple who has celebrated many years of marriage…

Someone lost a bunch of weight…

In all these scenarios, the outcome could go either way, right? But, right now, acknowledge the fact that all these people that you know, survived what at first seemed mighty impossible. Celebrate! Rejoice! Smile! Embrace it!

So, add your numbers and I'll add mine, and together we have a nice little group of miracles! Now, if we go really conservative and say that 100,000 people in each state can come up with the same number of miracles – well, that's a lot of good news action going on!

My point in all this is … do not give up hope. Ever. Nothing is impossible for God. Miracles happen every day. They do! God is busy every day. And they seem to happen to all kinds of people – the rich, the poor, regardless of race, age, sex, religion. And it can happen to you. Have hope.

Faithful reminder

The Lord's unfailing love and mercy still continue. Fresh as the morning, as sure as the sunrise. The Lord is all I have, and so in Him I put my hope (Lamentations 3:22-24).

My pastor/husband made a good point in his sermon last Sunday. He was explaining about how he keeps track of our finances on a spreadsheet and mentioned how we spent less money this year than the year before. But that wasn't the good news. The good news was looking at all those columns and rows of numbers and realizing that God had indeed provided by the thousands of dollars worth. Food. Water. House. Clothes. Car payments for sure, but also unexpected expenses like car repairs and medical expenses. And there were vacations and entertainment and gifts. Everything … everything we needed somehow got paid for. Did we worry about any of those things during the year? You bet. We all wonder, some people wonder week to week – where will the money come from? Yet here we are, into another year, still eating and drinking and maintaining a life.

All we have needed, God's hand has provided. Great is His faithfulness. Just look back over your old check register or bank statements or day planner. How much of what you worried about has been taken care of and in the past? Thank God!

Intentional focusing

Let the morning bring me word of Your unfailing love, for I have put my trust in You. Show me the way I should go, for to You I entrust my life (Psalm 143:8).

Intentional focus. I'm talking about that time (yes, time) when we choose to shut out the world and all other distractions, turning our thoughts to one thing, whether for a moment or a minute or more. You might have recently done that very thing around the family dinner table before you began eating. Purposefully thinking about thankfulness, praise, or a plea – and nothing else. Prayer. Turning our thoughts toward God.

When I had little ones in the house (I was a foster mom and an adoptive mom), I had children's mealtime prayers written out on index cards. Every day at dinnertime, I would shuffle them up, fan them out, and say, "Pick a prayer! Any prayer at all!" And it wasn't long before we all had them memorized. I wonder if any of them still remember: "Thank You, God, for daily bread. For apples and cherries red..." It was probably nice for them to have a reminder or a prompt from a card.

At another point in my life, those of you who knew me back when I was very shy and introverted, I was called upon at church to participate in healing prayer. That required being hooked up with a microphone, getting up in front of the whole church at the appointed time in the Sunday morning service, and leading the congregation in intercessory prayer as the requests came forward. Yeah, I know. Eek! No cue cards here! How could I ever be brave enough to be in this spontaneous- "oh-my!" prayer situation? Only God knows. But, wow, what a wonderful thing happened to me. I relied on God more than ever. Not knowing what prayer request would come up front, there was no way to prepare. God *had* to show up in the here and now, and show up He always did with just the right words. Many times "I" would reference a Scripture verse I had recently read. It just seemed to pop right into my head.

(The Sovereign Lord has given me an instructed tongue,
to know the word that sustains the weary. – Isaiah 50:4)

I don't think this verse from the Holy Bible was meant exclusively for Isaiah, because I think they sometimes apply to me. And if they sometimes apply to me, might they not also sometimes apply to you?

My intercessor is my friend as my eyes pour out tears to God;
on behalf of a man he pleads with God as a man pleads for his friend.
Job 16:20

God has mercy and compassion on all His people; faithful to all generations. Unchanging. The same God that spoke, helped, healed and gave strength to those in the Bible, is the same living God we have today.

So, verses from a recent Scripture reading, or a line from a song, or from a daily devotional – one sentence or phrase that stands out – can be turned into a prayer for someone, and it can be written down in a note card. Try this. Instead of saying "I am praying for you," actually write out a two or three sentence prayer. For a more powerful effect, insert the person's name into it. Prayers of thanks. Prayers for strength. Prayers for help.

Prayer is powerful and effective. Here are some sample verses I have used:

- Though You have made (_____) see troubles, many and bitter, You will restore (_____'s) life again; from the depths of the earth You will again bring (_____) up. You will increase (_____'s) honor and comfort (_____) once again. – Psalm 71:20-21

- When the Lord saw (_____), His heart went out to (_____) and He said, "Don't cry." – Luke 7:13

- I will turn the darkness into light before them and make the rough places smooth. These are the things I will do; I will not forsake (_____). – Isaiah 42:16

Dressing the part

Clothe yourselves with the Lord Jesus Christ, and do not think about how to gratify the desires of the sinful nature (Romans 13:12).

Never in all my life, would I have ever thought that I would someday participate in being in a skit or drama. I have always been way too shy! But life has its surprises and twists and turns, and a day came when I did start playing a role in a small five-minute skit for a Sunday morning message. And then another. And yes, then playing larger roles much to my own surprise! From bag lady to Mary Magdalene, I have dressed up and played a role.

I have to admit, aside from the part of worrying if I can memorize all the lines, there is a fun, playful side to me that really enjoys dressing up and pretending to be somebody else. I put the costume on and think about the words I'm going to be saying, and how that character might feel, and I am somehow braver than the shy Julie, when I was wearing Julie clothes.

I've read that is also a good way to change out of a bad habit, like for dieting, you get it in your head how a healthy, slimmer person acts and thinks and you choose to behave like that. *Act* like a healthy person. Healthy, "good weight" people don't grab a king-size candy bar at the checkout every time they go to the store. You put on that persona, and choose not to do it either.

I'm just wondering if that can work in other areas of life. I am thinking specifically about the Bible verse in Romans 13:12, "Clothe yourselves with the Lord Jesus Christ, and do not think about how to gratify the desires of the sinful nature."

Can I mentally "put on"/clothe myself with the good character of Jesus, and start *acting* that way? To no longer be clothed in my Julie clothes, so to speak, to behave differently knowing what Jesus calls us to do (love my neighbor as myself).

I'm going to get "dressed UP" today. I'm going to try to think about the words Jesus might use and what He might feel. I'm going to try to hang up my Julie clothes.

Birds of a feather

Every day they continued to meet together in the temple courts. They broke bread in their homes and ate together with glad and sincere hearts (Acts 2:46).

Since my move to another place to call home, I joined a knitting group. It's nice to spend time with people who enjoy the same things. They have experience in some of the many problems that "this knitting novice" can get into, because they have run into the same problems before. They have learned and grown from the same problem and are able to help me through it as well. Whether it's a dropped stitch (eek!) or a difficult to understand part of a pattern, they share their knowledge, their experiences in the journey, and are able to not only commiserate with my frustration, but can walk alongside me and help me see it through.

The same can be said of the weight awareness group I also joined. Although we don't often have bragging rights to great weight loss, we are all there together keeping each other accountable and sharing in each other's struggles. We travel this up-and-down road together. We are of value to one another in this journey.

And I guess that's why it's so important to share our stories. Whether it's something as simple as knitting or of grander scale such as weight loss or job loss or loved one loss. When you share your experience, it helps someone else be brave enough to face their circumstances. There's nothing worse than thinking you are the only one, not only with this problem, but thinking you're only one who can't handle the problem.

We are all survivors of something. What have you survived (or still surviving)? Are you willing to smooth the pathway for another? If you can send a note of encouragement, then do so. If you can cook up a meal and drop it off, please do. If you like to chat on the phone, then pick it up and call someone. If music touches your heart, bring the beautiful, healing qualities of music and song to one who could use some respite. Whether you eat or drink or whatever you do, do it as unto the Lord. May that be your inspiration for today.

Take this longtime burden, Lord

If it is possible, as far as it depends on you, live at peace with everyone (Romans 12:17).

I've been thinking a lot lately about strained relationships. It could be a friend or co-worker. Or it could be someone "closer" like a relative. Whether it's a parent, sibling or child, there's tension, stress, strain, distance, coolness … dysfunction. Our expectations of what the relationship should look like, feel like, act like seems far off and unattainable. We wrestle time and time again with what should be.

We live in a broken, sin-torn world.

Jesus said, "In this world, you will have trouble" (John 16:32).

"There is no difference, for all have sinned and fall short of the glory of God" (Romans 3:23).

We all have been traumatized in one way or another by the sin of such a world. The only view we really know of the situation is our own. Do we really think we know what the other person had to go through in this life? What personal, emotional struggles they deal with day after day, and most likely, struggling to keep secret.

We will all be much better at loving when we get to heaven. For now, maybe we should be most concerned about God's love and acceptance, approval and praise, than of other humans, even family members (John 5:44). Sometimes relationships can indeed be mended. Praise God! But there is also a reality that some relationships just can't, this side of heaven. Our cold, distant, separate ways are a result of a broken world. It's sad, but it's true. Not all relationships are beautiful, warm, nurturing, closely connected, and committed … not even family. We can't fix everything. Sometimes we need to let go, say goodbye to it, *and let God.* But then be ready when He does act. Be merciful and forgiving to everyone, giving *all* the benefit of the doubt, assume we don't know the whole story, and be at peace, loving and serving God and whatever people God brings into our daily life.

Do you know someone in this situation? Encourage them today that they don't need to be a doormat. There is such a thing as healthy boundaries. They don't need to fix it all. Being Christian doesn't mean getting everything all perfectly right all the time. It's a lot of falling down and getting back up, and trusting God is up to something beyond our understanding. Be still and wait upon the Lord. Some things just aren't up to you.

It's not what you think

Have you not heard? Long ago I ordained it. In days of old I planned it; now I have brought it to pass (Isaiah 37:26).

You just never really know when God is going to use you. Oh, you think you know what you have planned for the day, and you think you know how it will probably turn out. You make changes and other choices based on ... what? Feelings? How often have you said, "I should go, but I really don't *feel* like it." Tired? Yeah, probably. Lots of us are tired, but stop and think what kinds of things really refresh and revive us. I'll tell you right now it's not the paperback book and bag of chips I'm always joking about. It's getting out among other living things – people, friends, and nature.

So, I planned my Monday like we all do. I had a small group lunch to attend in Grand Rapids. And I also had an evening meeting in that area. So I planned on doing some window shopping and finding a nice place to have coffee and read while I passed the time in between. Now, there were only going to be three of us at the lunch, so I could have convinced myself it was too far of a drive. And I could have lived without wandering stores and coffee shops. I mean, it does sound a little, well, sorry, but not worth the effort. Have you ever felt like that? But God had other plans. "Love neighbor as yourself" plans. And He said, "Go!"

Lunch time turned out to be a mission trip of support and love and encouragement for my two dear friends. Both of them really needed to talk. Both of them really needed to be heard. We all need a safe time and place to spew out poisonous thoughts ... that in itself has healing power. Sometimes, I don't know what to say. I don't know exactly how to bring comfort. But I know the One Who can. And so we pray...

The rest of my afternoon? Well, let me tell you, I thought I'd really be struggling to fill in the time until that evening meeting. But how wonderful and delightful to not hurry through some familiar stores, I looked over every plant and flower, wandered up and down aisles, and sat in a sunny corner with coffee and a book and watched traffic and people. Ordered a delicious salad for supper and enjoyed a leisurely meal by myself. Oh my, what a surprise blessing to my life! It sure looked mundane first thing in the morning. But it turned out to be peaceful, joyful, and purposeful.

If your day starts out looking routine and ordinary, well, don't you give up hope. God can surprise you, too, with peace, joy, and purpose. Watch for it!

Multi-tasking

So whether you eat or drink or whatever you do, do it all for the glory of God (1 Corinthians 10:31).

Multi-tasking. I'm through with it. I no longer see the benefit. All I know is that while I'm doing one thing, I am distracted by thoughts of what else needs to be done. My mind drifts and instead being fully present and paying attention to what I am doing, I find myself doing a half-hearted job because of what I could be doing next. You don't really do two things at once. There's just short, two second spurts of focus from one to another and back again. Whether it's work to be done around the house or outside or notes to write or calls to make, I find my mind wandering to other things while I'm doing them.

Mopping the floors this morning. Is it really such a chore, or do I make it so? I like the smell of clean. I like how it looks and feels. And I like doing a good job. But with other thoughts vying for my attention, I tend to miss corners or walk over what I just did. Plus my anxiety increases as I think about all the jobs on my to-do list. You get the picture. One thing at a time is going to be my new motto. I'm going to do the best I can with what I've got at the moment and seek pleasure from it looking for the blessing in it, and be grateful. No more racing and rushing around in my mind tiring myself out with just weary thinking. Whether it's cooking dinner with relish or drinking iced tea and working on a jigsaw puzzle, don't miss the blessings. There is a time for everything under heaven. There is time.

A contented sigh

Surely You have granted him unending blessings and made him glad with joy of Your presence (Psalm 21:6).

The grass is always greener ... you know how the old saying goes. Which means *your* grass can appear greener to someone else. But how can that be? I'm of sound mind and body. I believe I'm in touch with reality. I can see and hear and touch. I believe I know what I'm talking about when I say somebody has it better than I do. Some have a greater sense of purpose than what I think I have right now. Some certainly have more money. Greater creature comforts. Better health and strength. But I am really amazed at the people who have less, and appear to be happier. And again I ask: how can that be?

In this worldly world of ours, you strive and strive and still it's not enough. Whether it's power or possessions or whatever, there's always more to be had. Where does it all end? When do you finally arrive at a place of sighing relief and contentment?

How about if we arrive *today*. How about we take a good look around the room we're sitting in right now and give thanks. How about we spend some time looking out the window and enjoying the whatever season of weather is out there. Open your fridge and your cupboards and praise God for His overabundant generosity. Take a walk through your neighborhood holding the hand of someone you love (yes, a dog leash counts!) and really relish every moment. Snuggle down in your bed tonight and rest your head on a pillow. Sigh and smile sweetly knowing God is standing guard over you yet again.

163

All grown up?

Create in me a clean heart, O God; and renew a right spirit within me (Psalm 51:10).

Seems like God has His work cut out for Him in renewing a right spirit within *me*. There are times when I think I'm doing a pretty good job of being Christian. I'm being nice, being helpful, going to church on Sunday morning. Sometimes I think I'm good enough ... right where I should be. I mean I know I'm not perfect, so where *I am* is good enough, right? I don't need to learn more, try more, or change more. I am what I am.

It sure sounds easier and more comfortable to think no more work has to be done. I mean, we've been having to grow and change all our lives. There were the school years, and landing a decent job years, then marriage and a house and babies and ... and some of us are just tired of the challenges and changes.

Somewhere, we have lost the excitement and anticipation of learning and growing. Remember the light bulb of understanding going off when you discovered something new at school? Or challenging yourself with something new at work and meeting that challenge and succeeding in what seemed impossible? Everything from reading new and different resources to going to new places and seeing new things on vacations; as your eyes were opened, your mind also found new ways to enjoy life, embrace life, praise this life.

O dear Lord, please keep working on me. Every morning, create a clean heart in me and renew a right spirit that I might truly live life to the fullest. Let me not be settled, satisfied, or content to think I've seen and heard and learned enough already. Keep challenging me to explore and wonder, look and see, consider all possibilities. And to seek You in all these things. Amen.

Journal a couple of your own thoughts ...

Rest … anywhere

Come with Me by yourselves to a quiet place and get some rest (Mark 6:31).

We are back from our week's retreat to Tennessee. Every morning, I got up early (yes, early, even on vacation) and sat out on this big porch with my cup of hot tea, my Bible, and a tablet. The mornings dawned sunny and bright some days, and sometimes there was a gentle rain falling. I would read my Bible and be drawn into this special time with our God. Amazing songs would pop into my head about the beauty and the wonders of God's created world. I felt transported. The air was fresh and clean. The view was lush and green and undisturbed. I would read and journal my meandering thoughts. It is a precious thing to sit with God unhurried. Nothing else I had to do. Nothing I had to hurry up and get started. I lingered with God. We were there in the silence. No agenda. No priorities. As thoughts came up, we considered them together. I sensed His words of assurance. His guidance about things I think about. Thoughts about how He likes things handled, which filled me not with guilt, but with possibility. It was a beautiful thing. I didn't want it to end, my beginning the day like that.

So I resolve to find that beauty in my own little piece of the world. My yard. There is a place to sit there. There is greenery and blue skies and puffy white clouds. I have my Bible and my tablet. There is nothing to stop me from spending time with Him.

Whether it's morning or evening, I wonder if you'll find a spot you find wonderful and take book and tablet in hand, and see where God takes you. He calls us all to rest. What are you allowing to get in the way of this precious gift?

Journal a couple of your own thoughts ...

Love the one you're with

For where two or three gather in My Name, there am I with them (Matthew 18:20).

Ever go to a meeting, Sunday morning church, a Bible study or "a something" and only a handful of people show up? And of the handful, only two read the material and are ready for discussion? If you're the one who has done all the prep work to lead the group, it can be disappointing. You feel like canceling ... you feel like cutting it short ... you feel like, "Why bother?"

I was taking another afternoon walk all alone today. I was thinking about all the people I miss being with. Either distance or work schedules keep us apart. I'm trudging through town and down the road, trying to enjoy the beautiful summer day. But like the group leader, I'm bummed. There should be more people here enjoying this.

But I keep walking and listening to my MP3 player and it's rocking out and I am stepping right along to the music. Then suddenly, a very peaceful, gentle, almost whisper-like song begins. It's about how beautiful Jesus is. It's a favorite of mine and it touches my soul. And I realize that in bemoaning all who aren't here, I'm overlooking the One Who is.

It made me think of all the times I've had to lead a meeting or a group discussion, or have been at a worship service where the attendance was low. I should have given my all to the one(s) there. The ones showing interest. The two or three gathered *with* me and not focus on the ones missing out.

I've learned a new lesson, Jesus. To love the ones you're with. Give my all. Whether it's a meeting, a Bible study ... or just a walk with You, Jesus.

Believing friends

When I pray I want to always thank You, God the Father of my Lord Jesus Christ, for the friends You have given me who have a genuine faith in Christ Jesus and a love for Your people. This faith and love spring from the hope that is stored up in heaven (Colossians 1:3-5).

It takes a lot of friends, each one having a special gift, to lift me up when I am down. Others spur me on and encourage me when I think I can't. More love me just the way I am. I have friends who bring me to my knees in laughter. Many more love Jesus like I do and love His people like He does and it's a wonderful thing to share this common thread woven through our hearts.

Despite any and all differences, there is a common bond that holds us as friends together ... we love Jesus dearly, and want to please Him, and bring glory to His name. And although we can't do it perfectly, with the help of one another, we continue to try to be good and kind and helpful in His strength and in His love that dwells within each one of us.

Our God is an awesome God. He blesses us with awesome friends. I am reminded of a song and I think the chorus goes something like this: we are one person; they are two alone; they are three together; they are four for each other. That really "sings" to me about being created individually, but moving forward together with common purpose: that the world may know Christ and the power of His resurrection.

Thanking God this morning for: those I can go to any time; those I can talk to and hold nothing back; who do not laugh at my dreams and failures; those who warn me of dangers and potential mistakes. But most of all, for all those friends journeying on this Christian walk with me every day in every way. Thanks be to God!

Journal a couple of your own thoughts ...

The gift of help

He asked the LORD, "Why have You brought this trouble on Your servant? What have I done to displease You that You put the burden of all these people on me? Did I conceive all these people? Did I give them birth? Why do You tell me to carry them in my arms, as a nurse carries an infant, to the land You promised on oath to their ancestors? (Numbers 11:11-12)

Life suddenly got busy and I had to be away from my normal routine and from my "normal" meditation and writing. A lot of it was work. A lot of it was service to others ... meeting others needs. And still, there seems to be so much more yet to do to bring things to completion.

I cannot carry all these people by myself; the burden is too heavy for me (Numbers 11:14).

I have to remind myself that I can't do it all. I can't fix everything, and I'm not meant to. I want to, but it's not all up to me.

The LORD said to Moses: "Bring Me seventy of Israel's elders who are known to you as leaders and officials among the people. Have them come to the tent of meeting, that they may stand there with you. I will come down and speak with you there, and I will take some of the power of the Spirit that is on you and put it on them. They will share the burden of the people with you so that you will not have to carry it alone (Numbers 11: 16).

I think about this Moses and how tired and overwhelmed he got. Does that sound like you? Too much on your plate? Much of it you didn't even ask for.

You're not meant to do it all. You're not meant to bring it to completion without help ... human help and spiritual power help. Enough help. Enough. Whatever the overwhelming burden, you don't have to carry it alone. The Lord sees your circumstances and sends help. Accept this gracious gift of help.

A special love

But while he was still a long way off, his father saw him and was filled with compassion for him; he ran to his son, threw his arms around him and kissed him (Luke 15: 20).

Famous star on a news program this morning was talking about his dad. A dad gone for quite some time now, but this star is hanging on to some artwork his dad did. He is reminiscing; remembering some good (and bad) times. He confesses they may not have had the best of relationships, but they were father and son.

Many dads of that era weren't real demonstrative in their love for their children. They didn't say and do things to encourage kids like we're taught to do now days. But in the midst of all these "souvenirs" of his dad's is a journal entry explaining how proud he is of his son. The son tears up.

Sometimes it's hard to believe someone loves us like that. That someone could be proud of us. When we look at ourselves, we see a history of mistakes and failures. Maybe we can squeak by with a feeling of, "I'm just okay. Nothing special. Just a regular person."

But the truth is, we all have a Father who sees something in each one of us to love and be proud of. How loved? How proud? Read the prodigal son story (Luke 15) and see:

- The father running when it's more dignified to walk
- Ordering the best robe, and the most significant ring and a party with the fattened calf.

Yes, even after all the mistakes and bad choices that son made. He is still loved. Still called son.

Do you feel like you're a long way off from God? Ever feel not good enough for that kind of love? No excuses. You are loved like that. It's in the Bible. Live in the love of the Father.

All your heart, soul, mind and strength

For whatever a man sows, that and that only is what he will reap (Galatians 6:7).

If one part of our body hurts, we hurt all over (1 Corinthians 12:26).

Garbage in, garbage out. Whether we're talking about what you feed your stomach or what you feed your mind, I think we can all painfully agree that what goes *in* dictates what comes *out*. There's no denying it: you plant a pumpkin seed, you're going to get a pumpkin and not a rose bush!

The 1 Corinthians verse reminds us that we are connected in more ways than one. We are not only physical beings, but also mental, emotional, spiritual, and relational beings. If we neglect one, the whole of us is somehow hurt or diminished or left not as strong. When we regularly nurture all aspects of our being, we are healthy, strong, happy and able. Let me give you an example.

When I eat junk food all day long, I physically become bloated, uncomfortable, cranky and sluggish. I don't feel like being helpful and nice to people. I don't want to do anything. Whatever I do seems to take so much energy. I can't focus on prayer or Scripture readings. The physical garbage affected my spiritual, emotional, and mental capacities.

On the other hand, when I eat a nutritious meal, take a walk in the fresh air, read a chapter in my Bible, and have coffee with a friend (nurturing all aspects of my being); all these working together make me a better whole person. When I'm a better whole person (when every part of my being is honored, cared for and respected), my whole body is happy and the living in love flows more naturally and without strain.

Does it sometimes feel too hard to love God and neighbor? Take a look at your whole being. What is getting nurtured and what needs a little more honor, respect, and care? It won't take as much as you think to bring yourself into balance. Be mindful of your whole being today. Take steps to tweak your daily pattern. Then love with all your heart, soul, mind and strength.

That the world may know

But when you proclaim His truth in everyday speech, you're letting others in on the truth so that they can grow and be strong and experience His presence with you (1 Corinthians 14:3).

Sometimes, I just feel better in my "prayer closet." Some may call it "quiet time." Some may just refer to it as praying. You know, being all alone, just me and God. I can read my Bible a little; tell God anything. I am safe, loved and accepted. God-thoughts enter my mind and I am uplifted. My prayer closet is a nice little place. Some days, I would like to stay there.

Keeping God all to myself. Relishing that special time together. So much more comforting and comfortable than dealing with people. Besides, sometimes it's just hard to explain what the experience is like in human terms. Being with God can be amazing!

There are some passages in 1 Corinthians 14 that refer to speaking in tongues, but a lot of it can also be applied to speaking or not speaking God's truths.

So, when you pray in your private prayer language, don't hoard the experience for yourself. Pray for the insight and ability to bring others into that intimacy (1 Corinthians 14:13).

What I read here is that we should ask for ways in which to reveal to others the awesomeness of time spent with God. Others should know about that "feel better" feeling I get from my special prayer time.

But if some unbelieving outsiders walk in on a service where people are speaking out God's truth, the plain words will bring them up against the truth and probe their hearts. Before you know it, they're going to be on their faces before God, recognizing that God is among you (1 Corinthians 14:25).

I have thought about this a lot as well. Especially in churches seeking growth. There are many things we do in a church service that has become old hat to the regulars, but to the newcomer, to the visitor, well, a helping hand close by to show which songbook to use, and which page the apostles creed is on, not to mention a friendly smile and a handshake, an invite to coffee hour *and* a little conversation with them there would go a long way. Certainly a sign that Jesus is among you. Your kindness could be a catalyst to softening their hearts toward God.

Whether someone is a new Christian or has years under their belt, living out acts of love and kindness are all aspects of the Christian walk that bring people to a greater sense of believing His loving presence is here with us.

Church – why I go

They devoted themselves to the apostles' teachings and to the fellowship, to the breaking of bread and to prayer (Acts 2:42).

All the believers were together (Acts 2:44).

I like to think of myself as *middle*-aged. I'm not hip, young, or cool. Not progressive. But heading toward that time in life when some are settling in to a new norm that has less energy than it once did, and are of an age where they have done a lot of what they had intended. I'm talking about church involvement here. The older generation has "served" its time in Sunday School and outreach programs … all the "do-do-doings" in the church. Many still have a heart for it, they are just running out of energy. But you can find them coming regularly, praying for people, worrying, wondering, and caring about folks. They desire to connect with the living God. The young people, the younger generation, well, where are they? I've heard they have their reasons. You've heard them, too.

But I'm going to stand up for the church, despite all its hypocrisy and people problems.

I wasn't raised in the church, but I like going to Sunday morning worship for many years of my adult life. I like the fact that it feels different than any other place I go. I like that the music is different, sometimes heavenly, sometimes haunting. Their words … *their words,* ring so true and are so comforting! I like the specialness of lighting candles up front, and ringing bells to start the service. I like having a confession prayer all printed out for me, because Lord knows, I don't like praying a confession on my own. I like to just sit and hear someone tell me about God. I like praying for others and praying in unison (there is an unmatched beauty in its rhythm). And I like considering the money God has sent my way, and how I can support something for His cause by giving a portion back. I like to look around and see familiar faces and share a wave and a smile across the room. It all has a "separateness" from my other days and places. A place to rest from the world and its pressures. I like spending time with people who love God, too. I like sharing in this different routine with them. I think I *need* this separateness. I need to believe there is something else besides this world. I welcome a glimpse of God and His heaven when I gather with other believers.

I hear and understand why the younger generation is not wanting to go to church. I know churches are full of stumbling, fumbling humans trying to make sense of (and express) the nature of Christ. But they sometimes get it right, too. There is a sense of belonging together and working together and loving, caring and laughing together. Maybe not so different from the real world after all. Except that as fellow believers, we can trust in a higher power to make things right. It's a time when we can join together and realize we don't have to have all the answers or get it all right on our own. There is Someone to praise for the beauty of nature. There is Someone Who can hear our weakest cry. There is Someone Who performs miracle upon miracle. And there is a place where you can share all of that … church. Where the real focus should be all about loving God and neighbor.

I sometimes struggle with finding the right words to express my prayer concerns. My singing along with others is much better than me singing alone – trust me on that one! And the beauty of stained glass windows, candles, huge crosses, banners … to turn my heart toward God. Then there's just a supernatural sensing/believing that God is there.

We were created to bring pleasure to God. And He is pleased and honored and delighted when we come together to worship Him. So come and worship Him.

Lord, I have some questions

The Lord is my Shepherd. I shall not want. He makes me lie down in green pastures. He leads me beside quiet waters. He restores my soul (Psalm 23:1-2).

O dear Lord, I pray for many, especially those on my growing prayer and concern list. I pray for words of hope, encouragement, good counsel, and strength that comes from You alone. All this devastating news all around us. It sure can be saddening to stop and care about it all.

Although our eyes do not see you, guide our faith into sensing You in the here and now. In the right here and right now. O Lord, transport us to a safe place where fear and pain don't have the upper hand. Some just found out there is a cancer. Some are going through draining treatments and therapy. Broken bones. Broken hearts. Back pain. Leg pain. Shoulder pain. Joblessness. Heart problems. Eye problems. Emotional overeating. You say to live in the present. Where are you, God? Where are Your words of hope and comfort?

Maybe we all need to slow down. Maybe we all need to talk to God a little more. Why so many burdens, especially when we *are* praying? What if this burden is sticking around? What if it's going to be this way for a long time? Where does the light for today come from? How do some persevere and overcome while others are challenged by problems and lie in misery day after day? What if our bodies are aging or damaged and there will always - from now on, in this life -

be an infirmary? What if hope for complete recovery on this side of heaven is in vain? Who am I then? Will daily pain describe me? Do we have too high of expectations of what good life should look like? What is a successful life really, but to walk humbly with our God. What if we spent time every day in prayer emptying ourselves of every burden? What if we spent a few moments here and there trying not to pray for anything, but just ask God to send a message? What if we spent a few minutes here and there appreciating the beauty of creation and the goodness we _do_ have? What if instead of creating a "good Christian should do" to-do list, as the occasion to help someone comes along, we help as God guides and supplies in that moment? What if this described a successful life? Could you live a life like that today despite your pain, your limitations, your health issues, your fears, your anger?

My prayer list of concerns is long and growing. Which tells me a lot of people are being made to slow down and reconsider what is really important.

The Lord is my Shepherd. I shall not want. He makes me lie down in green pastures. He leads me beside quiet waters. He restores my soul. (Psalm 23:1-2) My soul. My soul is what is important. My spirit. He tends to the condition of the spirit inside us.

A lot of people are struggling through this world of the tangible. But there is another place to focus.

Lord, we believe you are here, present. Although our eyes do not see you, our faith senses you.

Faith is being sure of what we hope for and certain of what we do not see (Hebrews 11:1).

Those of us who are older know we aren't ever going back to that 20-year-old body. Those who have suffered horrific battles through treatments may be some better than they were, but not 100 percent.

What is going to define us now, now that our bodies are a little weaker, or finances a little smaller, or relationships have fallen apart and drifted? Do these losses in life take the grandstand and define us now or is there something more to us, more *in* us?

In this earthly journey, every body, *everybody*, is having ups and downs. But do not be discouraged and do not be afraid. Loosen up on such high expectations, especially if you're not feeling well (physically, mentally, emotionally, financially, spiritually). Give yourself a break. You don't have to be happy-go-lucky every day, and you don't have to be down in the mouth everyday. Do the best you can with every day as it comes, and **lean into God every day**. That, my friend, is successful living.

For sure!

I remain confident of this: I will see the goodness of the LORD in the land of the living. Wait for the LORD; be strong and take heart and wait for the LORD (Psalm 27:13-14).

O dear Lord, I lift up this quiet time to You. I seek You in all areas of my life. Forgive me those things I still hold so tightly. I trust in Your orderly, growing process. I do want You to be Lord, Master, Ruler, King of my life and I want that to feel safe and not fearful of domination in an ugly way. You are a good, loving and caring Father God. I can rest in You. Thank You for Your Word that reminds me it is better to walk with You. Life will be more steadfast, no matter what happens, because I know You are a stabilizing force. You are an Anchor. You are a Rock. You are the stronghold of my life. I will not be tossed about on the angry sea of circumstances as long as I keep my heart, soul, mind and strength focused on You. I know You can do anything. I know You can handle anything. I know You turn everything into good. I trust in Your Word. I trust You as Ruler of both heaven and this present earth. I believe You to be faithful. I believe You to be Almighty. Of whom shall I fear? Again and again You direct my steps, whether daytime or night, whether in the midst of the good or the unpleasant, Lord, I believe in Your loving, concerned, steadfast character to preserve my life through it all. It is possible to know and experience Your great love in the here and now. Praise God! Praise God! We can taste and see that You are good! In the awesome privilege of our Savior's Name. Amen.

ABOUT THE AUTHOR

Julie Crane is the author/creator of Intermissions for Hope – a notes and card ministry and blog site. She spends her time designing whimsical note cards and sending words of encouragement to people far and wide. Her blog postings inspire others to have renewed hope in God. She is also regularly involved in Michigan Presbyterian Pilgrimage, an ecumenical 72-hour getaway for those in need of spiritual refreshment. Although this is her first book in print, she has written thousands of note cards to love, support and encourage others along their journey!

Julie lives in mid-Michigan with her pastor husband, Scott and their two cats. She's a mom, stepmom, and a Navy vet. Dramatist. Speaker. Small group leader too. And like you, a beloved child of God. She enjoys reading, knitting, walking the wooded trails, and eating ice cream.

Read more encouraging posts at my blogsite:
www.intermissionsforhope.blogspot.com

36920499R00110

Made in the USA
Lexington, KY
10 November 2014